# Investing in the Age of AI

# Investing in the Age of AI

A Guide to Smart Investing, AI-Driven Tools, and the Future of Financial Strategy

**Dr. Elias van Rothenstein**

**Mindful Pages**

Published in 2025

ISBN: 9789371343817 (PB)
ISBN: 9789371341509 (eBook)

*Published by*

**Mindful Pages**
*Imprint of Alpha Editions LLC*
312 W. 2nd St #1834
Casper, WY 82601, USA

# Content

# Introduction
# Rethinking the Investor's Edge

The image of the investor from decades past now seems almost quaint—belonging to another time, another rhythm. Once revered for gut instinct, long nights poring over ticker tapes, and the oral passing-down of market lore, the traditional investor embodied something closer to an artisan than a technician. Wealth was sculpted, not calculated. Success often depended less on formal models than on one's capacity to perceive what others overlooked—to move swiftly, with quiet conviction, while the rest of the world hesitated. Back then, intuition was king. But that era, however romantic, has largely receded into memory. The rules of the game have changed, and critically, so have the players. The edge is no longer, strictly speaking, human.

Artificial Intelligence has not simply entered the investment world as another helpful tool to enhance decision-making. It has redrafted the script entirely. Today's markets are shaped, even dominated, by systems capable not only of lightning-fast computation, but of learning, adapting, and—perhaps most disconcertingly—interpreting. These machines do more than execute. They observe, they anticipate, they act—and in doing so, they're quietly redrawing the contours of what it means to invest. In such a reality, the essential question emerges: what, if anything, is the investor's role now? Are we collaborators with these systems, or merely competitors in a game we no longer fully understand?

This book begins with a proposition that may provoke discomfort, or possibly ignite clarity: the human investor must evolve. Not in defiance of AI, nor under its shadow, but in dynamic relationship with it. This isn't a lamentation about humanity's waning dominance, nor a cheer for silicon ascendancy. Rather, it is a strategic and philosophical reckoning with a deeply altered reality. How does one maintain agency, discernment, and genuine perspective in a marketplace increasingly governed by entities that do not rest, second-guess, or succumb to the flaws that define us?

To truly understand this shift, one must appreciate the broader arc of financial innovation. The journey from ticker tapes to Bloomberg terminals, from handshakes with brokers to the ubiquity of ETFs, tells a story of progressive abstraction. And yet, even through all these iterations, it was still the human who stood at the helm—processing, interpreting, deciding. That dynamic has begun to reverse. Today, algorithms read earnings reports in milliseconds, gauge sentiment in a CEO's voice through vocal stress analysis, and adjust portfolio weightings based on satellite-fed data flows from global shipping routes. These systems don't wait for confirmation. They forecast.

Yet what makes AI so formidable isn't merely its speed or its scale. It's the alienness of its cognition. It identifies patterns no person could trace, constructs order where we see only noise, and operates unburdened by fear, greed, ego, or fatigue. In areas where our judgement stumbles, it thrives. Which brings us to the heart of the matter: if machines surpass us in processing, prediction, and emotional neutrality, what exactly is left for the human investor?

That question sits at the centre of this book.

*Investing in the Age of AI* is neither a eulogy for the instinctive investor nor a hymn to algorithmic mastery. It is a call to reimagine the act of investing itself—not just as a technical pursuit, but as a form of thinking, of perceiving, even of identity. The investor who endures and excels in this new age will not do so by replicating machine logic, but by embracing the distinctly human faculties that cannot be programmed. Curiosity. Ethical discernment. The capacity for ambiguity. Emotional depth. These are no longer peripheral—they are fast becoming central.

We begin, in Chapter One, by casting a clear eye on the present state of traditional investing. *The End of the Traditional Investor* lays bare the ways in which foundational strategies—value investing, technical indicators, and other once-reliable frameworks—are being steadily outpaced or redefined by AI's relentless capacity. Investing has shifted from story-driven intuition to a battle of informational fluency. So where, now, does human acumen fit?

Chapter Two, *What AI Sees That You Don't*, offers a glimpse into AI's perceptual reach. Whether it's interpreting satellite imagery of car parks to infer retail trends or analysing word choice in earnings calls to detect executive confidence, AI sees with a breadth and subtlety we can scarcely fathom. But even here, its clarity has blind spots. Without emotion, there is no context. Without imperfection, no insight into the irrational undercurrents that shape markets. For all its genius, AI remains fundamentally incomplete.

*Human Intelligence Reimagined*, Chapter Three, shifts the focus from observation to reinvention. What intellectual virtues are ours alone? We explore metacognition, the moral calculus of decision-making, and the interpretive nuance that no neural net can replicate. In a world saturated with data, reflection—not reaction—becomes the rarest and most valuable skill.

With Chapter Four, *Portfolio by Algorithm*, the conversation turns practical. From robo-advisors to digital twins simulating wealth trajectories, the new toolkit is extensive and readily accessible. Yet owning these tools is not the same as wielding them wisely. Understanding their assumptions, their blind spots, their utility and limits—that is where human mastery still matters.

Chapter Five, *Wealth as an Information System*, takes a conceptual turn. What if capital is no longer best understood as a static asset but as dynamic data—flux, signal, pattern? In this framing, the investor becomes less a picker of stocks and more a reader of currents, a navigator of meaning in motion.

We enter more intimate terrain in Chapter Six, *Emotional Algorithms and Psychological Traps*. Emotion has long been cast as investing's great liability. But what if it's also its secret strength? We examine how behavioural patterns are exploited—by platforms, by algorithms, even by our own wiring—and how emotional intelligence, rather than being suppressed, might be strategically refined and applied.

Chapter Seven, *AI-Powered Futures*, maps the expanding frontier. From cryptocurrencies shaped by machine sentiment analysis to ESG data reinterpreted through visual recognition algorithms, asset classes themselves are being restructured. This is not trend-chasing. It is survival in shifting terrain.

The philosophical heart of this work lies in Chapter Eight: *Philosophy of Risk in an Automated Age*. Too often, risk is reduced to a number—a line on a graph, a quantifiable metric. But true risk is existential. It is about acting under uncertainty, absorbing consequence, bearing exposure. As AI hedges every calculable edge, humans must rediscover what it means to risk meaningfully, even nobly.

In Chapter Nine, *Building Your AI-Enhanced Investment Philosophy*, the lens turns inward. This isn't about asset allocation. It is about coherence—crafting a worldview that integrates values, strategy, and a grounded understanding of one's place in the system. Investment, after all, is never neutral. It is a reflection of what we believe about the world and our agency within it.

Finally, Chapter Ten, *The Investor of the Future*, looks ahead. In a field increasingly saturated with intelligence—artificial and otherwise—what defines excellence? Not omniscience. Not precision. But adaptability. Ethical clarity. A systems-level consciousness. The next great investor will not be the lone genius, but the architect of a thoughtful, responsive, and emotionally resilient approach.

This book makes no promises of market-beating returns. It offers no shortcuts or magic ratios. What it does offer is something rarer and, perhaps, more enduring: orientation. A way to think. A framework for staying grounded and agile amid change.

To invest in the age of AI is not to surrender our humanity. Quite the opposite—it demands we deepen it, sharpen it, and wield it with greater care.

That is the edge we retain. And that is where our journey begins.

# Chapter 1
# The End of the Traditional Investor

Once, the investor was seen less as a technician and more as a kind of market whisperer—someone who read the ebbs and flows not only through data, but through feel. Investing was something you inhabited, not just analysed. It was a craft, with its own rhythms, idioms, and quiet rituals. A blend of temperament and theory. Buffett's steady hand, Graham's principled caution, the careful scribbles of technical analysts sketching resistance lines as though they were maps through fog. To invest, in that older vision, was to interpret—a practice part empirical, part poetic.

But time, unbothered by nostalgia, has moved on. And it hasn't asked for permission. Algorithms, indifferent to intuition and untroubled by sleep, now shape much of the financial landscape. They don't guess. They don't pause. They process and execute with ruthless precision. Where an investor once leaned on instinct—waiting for signals to align, for the air to shift—the machines have no such need. The data is enough. In fact, it's everything.

This chapter traces that transformation—not simply a change in methodology, but a more fundamental reshaping of what constitutes authority in the financial realm. We're not just swapping tools here; we're rewriting what it means to "know" a market. Human intuition, long celebrated, now jostles for space with systems that digest data faster, broader, and with far fewer blind spots.

It didn't happen overnight. For decades, investing was a narrative-rich terrain where gut feel and lived experience counted for much. The lore of the floor trader, the glory of the lone stock-picker, the mystique of the contrarian thinker—they dominated. Figures like Soros spun theories of reflexivity, while Schwager's interviews with "market wizards" hinted at something near alchemical. But beneath this romantic façade lurked a limitation: human cognition. There's only so much a brain—however brilliant—can track, especially in an age of swelling datasets and globalised speed.

At first, the shift was subtle. Spreadsheets became more complex. Risk models flirted with Monte Carlo simulations. Fund managers ran quiet experiments with quant overlays. It felt like augmentation—tools to sharpen judgement, not replace it. But then the pivot came. Slowly, then decisively, code began to lead. Quantitative firms like Renaissance Technologies didn't just operate faster; they operated differently. They treated the market as a computational problem, not a story. Their strategies weren't written—they were trained.

Plenty scoffed. Real investing, critics claimed, wasn't about squeezing signals from statistics. It was about value. About understanding companies. About conviction. But the scoreboard said otherwise. Quant funds ascended. Passive flows overtook active ones. The classic image of the charismatic portfolio manager faded into sepia.

The tremors of this shift unsettled traditional disciplines. Take value investing—a once-stalwart philosophy now, many argue, adrift. The metrics that once uncovered underpriced gems are now processed, arbitraged, and often neutralised by machines long before a human analyst finishes their morning coffee. Technical analysis? Its once-clever geometries now look almost childlike next to multi-variable machine learning models that detect patterns across timeframes, asset classes, and sentiment channels. In short: the old playbooks are being outpaced by entities that don't even play the same game.

It's tempting to blame exogenous shocks—interest rate distortions, a glut of capital, or monetary interventions. But that lets us off the hook too easily. Perhaps the truth is more direct: these approaches were built for a world where humans made the trades. That world, increasingly, does not exist. Machines initiate and manage the majority of trading flows. They read reports, dissect filings, scour forums. They don't sleep, hesitate, or waver. Their version of instinct is iteration.

But the real challenge isn't just speed. It's the nature of machine cognition. AI does not think, at least not in the way we do. It doesn't concern itself with story arcs or moral weight. It optimises. It adjusts. It rewards success and penalises failure with the cold efficiency of a function. Its "judgement" is probabilistic. Its "experience" is training cycles. In this worldview, investing is no longer an act of belief. It is an act of architecture. Strategy becomes structure. And the investor? Less prophet, more builder.

One sees this most clearly in the manipulation of time. High-frequency trading firms battle in microseconds. Infrastructure investments target latency reduction with almost military obsession—microwave networks, server co-location, algorithmic choreography. The race is no longer about who understands the market, but who can get there first. And in such a race, the patient analyst—once seen as wise—now feels miscast.

Yet it would be a mistake to declare the death of the human investor. The myth, yes—that of the lone operator with a sixth sense for stocks—that's largely finished. But the role itself? It's simply evolving. The competitive edge no longer lies in raw interpretation but in design. In engineering systems that incorporate machine insight while preserving distinctly human faculties. Qualities like ethical reasoning, strategic foresight, contextual nuance.

This chapter attempts to chart that evolution. We'll delve into why gut-led decision-making lost its edge. Explore how legacy strategies, once dominant, now falter. We'll probe how machines reframe risk—not as danger, but as deviation—and why that reframing matters. We'll explore speed not merely as executional advantage, but as an ideology. And we'll consider: what does it mean to think slowly, deeply, in a world that thinks faster than we can blink?

The point here is not to stir wistfulness or to suggest capitulation. It is to locate clarity in a disorienting landscape. To invest with a mindset frozen in another era is not just quaint—it's costly. What's required is not nostalgia, nor blind faith in algorithms, but something altogether more demanding: a new inner architecture. One that respects the strength of machines while guarding against their blind spots. That knows when to lean in, and when to step back.

This is not the death knell of human investing. It is the threshold of a richer, more deliberate practice. One where the human role is redefined—not by retreating from machines, but by coexisting with them. And in that tension, that careful balance, lies perhaps the last true edge we possess.

## From Intuition to Automation

There was a time when markets were arenas for human intuition. The best investors were not those with the most computing power or the most complex models, but those with experience-honed instincts and the ability to perceive opportunity in ambiguity. Traders leaned over ticker tapes, analysts parsed quarterly reports with a red pen and a magnifier's eye, and conviction—the unquantifiable but palpable sense that a move was right—was a legitimate form of capital. But if the defining trait of the 20th-century investor was intuition, the defining trait of the 21st is something altogether different: *automation.* The gut has given way to the grid.

To understand this shift is to grasp one of the most important transformations in the modern history of finance. It is not merely technological—it is cognitive. It is a shift in *who* does the deciding, *how* decisions are made, and *what* knowledge is considered valid. Where once the mind of a seasoned investor was seen as an irreplaceable edge, we now see increasing reliance on systems that learn, optimise, and adapt with a precision no human can rival. The mythology of the intuitive investor has not disappeared, but it has been subordinated—filtered, audited, and often overridden by machine logic.

The roots of this transformation run deep. For much of the 20th century, the act of investing was characterised by information asymmetry and slow-moving markets. Prices were set by supply and demand, yes, but also by narrative, sentiment, and interpretation. The tools of the trade were limited—financial statements, economic forecasts, and eventually, basic computing models. Analysts had time to think. Managers had room to breathe. Entire strategies were built on the assumption that human insight was the arbiter of value. The famed investors of the era—Buffett, Templeton, Lynch—were revered not just for their returns, but for their *judgement.* Their reading of markets was not just mathematical; it was philosophical.

But as technology began to accelerate, so too did the nature of competition. The introduction of electronic trading in the 1970s, followed by the proliferation of personal computing and spreadsheet modelling in the 1980s and 1990s, slowly began to erode the monopoly of human discretion. By the early 2000s, hedge funds and proprietary trading desks were using quantitative strategies not only to evaluate risk, but to determine asset allocation and execute trades. Today, that early wave has grown into a tsunami. According to estimates by JP Morgan, as much as 60 to 70 percent of trading volume in US equities is now driven by algorithms. Human traders have not vanished—but in many corners of the market, they have become spectators rather than actors.

This shift is not simply about speed or scale. It is about *how intelligence itself is defined and deployed.* Intuition, by its nature, is context-driven. It relies on patterns of recognition developed over years—sometimes decades—of lived experience. It is subtle, nuanced, and often deeply personal. Automation, by contrast, does not intuit. It models. It ingests data, identifies probabilistic relationships, and acts in real time, unencumbered by memory, emotion, or ambiguity. Where intuition interprets, automation calculates. Where intuition hesitates, automation executes.

To many traditional investors, this feels alienating. The language of finance has shifted: from narrative to model, from gut to gradient descent, from balance sheets to big data. Consider a portfolio manager trained in classical fundamentals. She may believe, correctly, that a particular company is undervalued based on earnings quality, management credibility, and sector positioning. But if her thesis takes six months to play out, and an algorithm can identify a 0.2% arbitrage in six milliseconds, she is not just playing a different game—she is playing on a different timeline. And increasingly, the market rewards the latter.

This is not to say that automation has made intuition obsolete. Rather, it has *redefined the role of intuition within a broader system of decision-making.* In many modern investment firms, human intuition is still valued—but it is viewed as one input among many, subject to validation by models and increasingly framed in probabilistic terms. A manager may have a "hunch," but that hunch will be tested against a Monte Carlo simulation, benchmarked against factor models, and constrained by automated risk parameters. What was once a primary mode of engagement is now often a secondary overlay, filtered through machine logic.

To appreciate the magnitude of this shift, one need only look at the rise of firms like Renaissance Technologies, Citadel, and DE Shaw—organisations whose internal cultures resemble research laboratories more than Wall Street trading floors. These firms operate not on conviction, but on computation. They don't just crunch numbers—they engineer entire epistemologies of decision-making, where knowledge is defined by predictive power, not narrative coherence. Their strategies are not built around quarterly earnings or CEO charisma, but around correlations, signals, and machine-learned inferences across massive, unstructured datasets.

The epistemic difference is profound. Traditional investors look for *why* something is undervalued. Quantitative systems look for *when* something statistically behaves in a way that is exploitable. The former seeks explanation; the latter seeks advantage. And in a market where billions of data points are processed every second, *advantage* increasingly belongs to those who can adapt to the informational environment, not merely interpret it.

Yet automation comes with its own limitations—and these are not trivial. Machines can model relationships, but they struggle with *meaning.* They can detect sentiment in a tweetstorm, but they cannot interpret moral nuance in an earnings call. They can simulate thousands of scenarios, but they cannot anticipate the ethical implications of their recommendations. This asymmetry—between computational capacity and contextual understanding—is one of the great tensions of modern finance.

It is also why the human investor is not extinct, but evolving. The future of investing is not binary: it is not intuition *versus* automation, but a careful synthesis of the two. The most effective investors in the coming decade will not be those who resist automation, nor those who blindly defer to it. They will be those who understand *how* and *when* to integrate machine intelligence into their decision frameworks—when to trust the model, and when to interrogate it.

This is already evident in the rise of hybrid strategies. Some of the most forward-thinking firms are now building teams that combine data scientists with behavioural economists, quantitative analysts with philosophers. The goal is not to replace the human element, but to recontextualise it: to use automation as a way to extend and augment intuition, not silence it. These teams understand that human insight, when disciplined by data and framed within systems thinking, can still generate unique and defensible advantages.

Indeed, one of the underappreciated truths of the automation revolution is this: intuition, when properly calibrated, may become *more valuable*, not less. In a world flooded with information and dominated by high-frequency execution, the capacity to *ask the right question*, to *frame the right problem*, and to *interpret uncertainty* through an ethical and strategic lens becomes a differentiator. Machines can optimise within parameters—but humans still define the parameters. Machines can adjust to volatility—but humans still interpret consequence. *That is the new frontier of intuitive thinking*—not as solo judgement, but as strategic architecture.

There is a final consideration, and it is not merely technical. As automation advances, we are confronted with questions that extend beyond efficiency and execution. What do we want markets to do? Who do we want them to serve? What risks are we willing to tolerate—not just statistically, but ethically? These are not questions a neural network can answer. They are questions for humans—and they require a form of intelligence that cannot be automated: reflective, moral, long-term thinking.

The shift from intuition to automation is not the end of human relevance in investing. But it is the end of a particular kind of heroism—the lone trader, the intuitive genius, the mythic investor who "just knows." What replaces it is more complex, more distributed, and more demanding. It requires humility, systems fluency, and a willingness to think differently about what it means to "know" the market.

And for those willing to make that leap, the rewards are not just financial. They are intellectual. They are strategic. And, most importantly, they are human.

## The Collapse of the Old Playbook

A generation ago, the most respected investors in the world read from the same book. Its pages were filled with principles honed by decades of empirical observation and common-sense reasoning. Buy low, sell high. Identify undervalued companies with durable competitive advantages. Watch the charts. Trust the patterns. At its core, the old playbook was built on the assumption that human perception—filtered through experience, discipline, and rationality—was the best tool for navigating financial markets.

That assumption no longer holds. The strategies that once underpinned institutional decision-making and personal wealth-building alike—*value investing*, *technical analysis*, and various hybrids thereof—have lost their predictive power and strategic potency in a market environment now shaped by artificial intelligence. These legacy frameworks, once considered evergreen, are being re-evaluated not because their logic is flawed, but because the context in which they operate has fundamentally changed.

The collapse of the old playbook is not the result of a single technological innovation or market anomaly. It is the outcome of a deeper structural transition—one in which the very fabric of price discovery, information processing, and behavioural feedback has been rewired. To understand why formerly successful strategies are now faltering, one must examine how AI is not merely replacing human inputs, but *displacing the assumptions* those strategies were built upon.

Start with value investing. Rooted in the teachings of Benjamin Graham and refined by investors like Warren Buffett, value investing relies on the principle that markets are inefficient in the short term but rational over the long haul. The approach assumes that intrinsic value—based on earnings, assets, and other fundamentals—can be estimated more accurately than the market does in the present moment. It presumes that eventually, the gap between price and value will close, and the patient investor will be rewarded.

But this presumption has been steadily undermined. The central thesis of value investing depends on inefficiencies that take time to correct. Yet today's markets, flooded with real-time data and governed increasingly by machine learning algorithms, have dramatically compressed the window in which such inefficiencies exist. AI-powered trading systems digest financial statements, analyse sentiment, compare cross-sector trends, and model macroeconomic data faster than any human analyst can react. A price anomaly that once lasted months may now correct itself in seconds.

Moreover, many of the valuation metrics that served as reliable signals in the past—low price-to-book ratios, high dividend yields, discounted cash flow models—are now less informative. Not because they've become incorrect, but because they are *no longer scarce.* Machine-readable datasets have commoditised these signals. When every institutional investor has access to the same metrics, processed by similar models, the edge disappears. Alpha migrates elsewhere.

The picture is no brighter for technical analysis, a methodology that seeks to forecast price movements through historical patterns, resistance levels, and volume indicators. For much of the 20th century, technical analysis offered a viable complement—or alternative—to fundamental strategies. Its core promise was visual: patterns on a chart could reveal human behaviour in aggregate, especially fear, greed, and herd psychology. The infamous head-and-shoulders formation, for instance, or Fibonacci retracement levels, were believed to capture the emotional cadence of markets.

Yet today, the behavioural substrate that gave technical patterns their power has changed. Human traders have been displaced by automated systems that do not feel emotion, do not observe patterns, and do not react in the same rhythm. A support line once assumed to represent a psychological price floor may now be breached not by sentiment, but by a model adjusting its parameters based on an external data stream—a subtle change in interest rate expectations, or a tweet with embedded geopolitical implications. Algorithms trade on correlations invisible to chartists. They exploit microsecond inefficiencies at a granularity human eyes cannot perceive. The result is a behavioural inversion: instead of predicting mass psychology, technical patterns are now prey to algorithmic triggers that neutralise or reverse their expected outcomes.

What we are witnessing is not merely a failure of specific strategies, but a breakdown of the environmental conditions that made those strategies viable. The old playbook was designed for markets where price reflected human cognition—slow, biased, yet interpretable. The new market reflects machine cognition—fast, pattern-driven, and increasingly opaque. AI systems do not see value in the same way. They model utility, momentum, correlation, and probability—not story, sentiment, or fundamental fairness. They act without narrative.

This has profound implications for how we think about edge. In the old paradigm, edge was about insight: seeing something others missed. In the current landscape, edge is about *architecture*: building systems that process information more completely, more quickly, and with less noise. The human role, once central, is now at risk of becoming interpretive rather than generative. Many institutional investors already function more like curators of models than independent thinkers with original theses. The portfolio manager has become part data scientist, part behavioural referee, part systems optimiser.

But this transition is not without internal contradiction. Despite their sophistication, AI models are still bounded by the data they are trained on. Their outputs are shaped by prior patterns and historical dynamics—which means they can misfire when the future fails to resemble the past. The 2020 pandemic and the 2022 energy shock both exposed such limitations. Models trained on decades of economic continuity struggled to interpret non-linear disruptions. When causality fragments and correlation breaks down, the machine becomes as blind as the human—only faster.

This fragility suggests that while the old playbook may be collapsing, the replacement is not infallible. It also reopens space for something more dynamic: *human-machine integration.* Rather than choosing between vintage heuristics and silicon-based analytics, the most forward-thinking investors are now working to develop a hybrid model of intelligence—one that acknowledges the limitations of both intuition and automation. They treat algorithms not as oracles, but as instruments. They read technical signals with scepticism, while also recognising that human behaviour has not disappeared—it has simply been refracted through a different set of feedback loops.

For example, behavioural finance—once a marginal discipline—has become a focal point for designing algorithms that anticipate irrationality. Rather than ignoring emotions, some AI systems now model them through proxy indicators: social media sentiment, option skew, or retail trading flows. This approach treats the market not as a machine to be deciphered, but as an evolving ecosystem where human tendencies still matter, but in increasingly indirect ways. Even value investing is being reimagined through machine learning, with firms like AQR incorporating high-dimensional data to identify quality factors that go beyond the traditional metrics.

What replaces the old playbook, then, is not a single strategy or formula, but a mindset shift. Success in the AI age will not depend on memorising principles or following expert scripts. It will depend on *framework thinking*: the ability to question assumptions, design systems, and evaluate models not only by their backtested performance, but by their adaptability and interpretability. This demands a deeper literacy—not just in finance, but in technology, ethics, and epistemology.

To invest effectively today is to ask better questions. Not just "Is this stock undervalued?" but "How is value being defined, measured, and acted upon in this environment?" Not just "What does the chart say?" but "Whose logic is shaping this chart—and can that logic be reverse-engineered or trusted?" It is not enough to observe patterns. One must understand who is writing them, and why.

The collapse of the old playbook should not be mourned. It should be understood as a signal: that the rules of the game are changing, and that clinging to legacy frameworks in a world governed by non-human intelligence is a strategic liability. But this collapse also creates space—for new strategies, new thinking, and new kinds of investors.

What endures is not the method, but the mindset: an investor must still strive to understand the market deeply, question received wisdom rigorously, and act decisively when conditions align. That has not changed. What has changed is the terrain on which these virtues are tested.

The future does not belong to those who remember the old rules best. It belongs to those who learn how to write new ones.

## The Rise of the Machine Mindset

Ask an experienced investor how they assess risk, and you're likely to hear about uncertainty, downside protection, capital preservation, or emotional fortitude in the face of volatility. Ask an AI system, and the answer will be expressed not in metaphors or narratives, but in numbers—distributions, matrices, loss functions, and expected values. The contrast is not cosmetic. It is foundational. *Machines do not think like us. They do not need to.* The machine mindset represents a radical reorientation of how financial decisions are made, not because it seeks better guesses, but because it operates from a different definition of intelligence itself.

This distinction—between how humans *feel* risk and how machines *model* it—is not a trivial divergence in style. It is a divide in epistemology. Traditional investment thinking has always been tethered to human cognition. Even when quantitative tools were used, they were often designed to support heuristics and frameworks derived from human intuition. Value investing, technical analysis, even modern portfolio theory—all were constructed within the limits of human perception and interpretive bandwidth. They assume that investors are boundedly rational agents, influenced by emotion, memory, and social context.

Artificial intelligence has no such constraints. When AI assesses risk, it does so from first principles that reflect a computational worldview. It does not rely on historical analogy or personal experience. It does not fear regret, overreact to losses, or overweight salient events. It operates with a mechanical neutrality that is both its greatest strength and, at times, its most significant vulnerability.

Consider how a deep learning model tasked with portfolio optimisation views the world. It doesn't "believe" in sectors or stories. It doesn't interpret CEO body language or read central bank minutes for tone. Instead, it ingests thousands of features—from macroeconomic indicators and earnings data to satellite imagery, credit card transaction volumes, and social media sentiment—and searches for statistical relationships that maximise a defined objective. This objective is encoded as a *loss function*—a mathematical representation of error or undesirability that the model seeks to minimise.

Where the human investor might frame a decision in terms of conviction ("I believe this company is undervalued"), the machine frames it as probability-weighted utility ("These inputs are associated with a statistically significant increase in return under these constraints"). This may sound coldly rational, but it is also profoundly liberating. The AI is not anchored by story. It is unburdened by ideology. It can detect faint patterns across vast, non-intuitive dimensions—patterns no human could see, let alone act upon in real time.

Yet this strength also reveals a philosophical fault line. *Machines "think" in terms of optimisation, not meaning.* Human investors frequently trade off risk for purpose—allocating capital to align with values, to support innovation, to avoid regret, or simply to sleep at night. AI has no such compass. It optimises for the objective it is given. If that objective is short-term alpha, it will pursue it relentlessly, regardless of whether the trades align with ethical or systemic sustainability. This creates a critical responsibility for human oversight—not to tell the machine *how* to invest, but to define *what it should care about.*

This is not a hypothetical concern. Consider the case of high-frequency trading algorithms that have, on occasion, triggered "flash crashes"—rapid, extreme price movements that defy fundamental logic. These systems were not malfunctioning. They were working *exactly as intended*—optimising for speed, order priority, and market microstructure. But their lack of broader contextual awareness led them to amplify instability rather than dampen it. They played the game better than any human could, but without understanding *why the game exists.*

This raises the deeper question: what does it mean to invest in a world where decision-making is outsourced to entities that do not understand risk as consequence, only as calculus?

To answer this, we must understand how AI conceptualises risk, opportunity, and optimisation—not metaphorically, but mathematically.

**Risk**, in the machine mindset, is often framed as variance, drawdown probability, or tail-event likelihood. These are not approximations of fear—they are abstractions of dispersion. A reinforcement learning agent managing a dynamic portfolio might learn that reducing volatility increases long-term reward only if the reward function penalises volatility explicitly. Otherwise, it may favour more volatile assets that offer higher expected returns. There is no intrinsic aversion to risk—only a sensitivity to how the reward system is structured.

This is a crucial departure from behavioural finance. Humans are notoriously loss-averse; they feel the pain of losses more acutely than the pleasure of equivalent gains. This shapes their investment decisions, often irrationally. Machines, however, treat gains and losses symmetrically unless otherwise instructed. This lack of emotional asymmetry allows for cleaner logic, but also increases the risk of *overfitting*—optimising for statistical artefacts that do not persist in live environments.

**Opportunity**, likewise, is not identified through thematic insight or qualitative assessment. It is located within multidimensional feature spaces. AI models detect patterns that correlate with future price changes, even when those patterns appear meaningless to humans. For instance, a model might discover that an increase in cloud computing job postings in certain zip codes predicts retail sales growth, which in turn correlates with the performance of consumer discretionary ETFs. This kind of connection—non-obvious, data-rich, high-dimensional—is where machines excel. They do not require interpretability to act; they require *predictive power.*

This creates a new kind of opacity. In the past, investment rationale was a core part of the decision process—used for both conviction and communication. Investors could explain their thinking. Machines often cannot. The internal logic of a deep neural network is notoriously difficult to decode. This "black box" problem introduces both regulatory and epistemic challenges: How do we trust a system whose decisions we cannot explain? And more importantly, how do we *learn* from it?

**Optimisation** is the final pillar of the machine mindset. Humans often make satisficing decisions—choices that are "good enough" given constraints like time, attention, and emotional tolerance. AI systems, by contrast, are relentless optimisers. They can test millions of strategies, iterate continuously, and adjust in real time to new inputs. This has made possible a class of investment tools that are adaptive in ways traditional models could never be. Yet this optimisation is often brittle. It performs brilliantly *within distribution*—when future conditions resemble past training data—but can fail catastrophically *out of distribution*. This makes the machine mindset powerful but vulnerable. It is a scalpel, not a shield.

The implications for human investors are significant. First, they must relinquish the illusion that intuition alone can compete with algorithmic intelligence. But they must also resist the temptation to defer entirely to machines. The goal is not to mimic the machine mindset, but to *understand it*—to grasp its logic, its blind spots, and its philosophical premises.

This means learning to think in systems terms. It means becoming literate in how objectives are defined, how data is weighted, and how models evolve. It also means reclaiming the role of ethical architect. The machine will do what it is told. It is up to the human to ensure that what it is told reflects not just statistical efficiency, but strategic and moral clarity.

One promising example of this hybrid thinking is the growing field of explainable AI (XAI), which seeks to make machine learning outputs interpretable to human decision-makers. In finance, this could allow investors to better understand *why* a model is recommending a particular allocation, and to challenge or adjust that reasoning if it conflicts with broader goals. Another frontier is the development of multi-objective optimisation frameworks, where models are trained to balance financial return with sustainability metrics, social impact, or long-term systemic resilience.

In other words, the rise of the machine mindset need not signal the decline of human agency. It signals the evolution of that agency into a new form—less centred on gut calls and more focused on system design. The future investor is not the lone analyst or charismatic trader. It is the *strategic orchestrator*—someone who understands how intelligence can be distributed, structured, and governed within a complex, machine-augmented environment.

To think like a machine is not to abandon humanity. It is to confront the limits of intuition with humility, and to supplement it with the best tools our civilisation has ever built for pattern recognition, probability estimation, and dynamic learning. But it is also to remember what machines cannot do: *value*, *prioritise*, *care*.

Risk, opportunity, and optimisation may be calculable. Meaning is not.

The machine mindset is rising. The human challenge is not to resist it, but to understand it—deeply, critically, and with the moral seriousness it demands. Only then can we invest not just intelligently, but wisely.

## When Speed Becomes Strategy

If investment decisions were once defined by depth of insight, today they are increasingly defined by *speed of execution*. Not because insight has lost its value, but because—on many fronts—it has lost its window. In markets now dominated by machines that can interpret, decide, and act within microseconds, the speed at which one can respond to information has, in many contexts, become the strategy itself. What used to be an operational feature of a well-run fund—efficient execution—is now a decisive competitive edge. The result is a profound reconfiguration of the investing landscape, where success hinges not merely on what you know, but on *how fast your systems can act on that knowledge.*

High-frequency trading (HFT) exemplifies this shift with almost surgical clarity. These are strategies that rely not on long-term theses or deep fundamental research, but on the exploitation of infinitesimal inefficiencies that exist for milliseconds at a time. They are executed not by humans, but by algorithms operating at speeds that border on the physically implausible. The archetype of the investor poring over earnings reports and macroeconomic forecasts has, in many asset classes, been displaced—functionally if not symbolically—by machines optimising for latency, network proximity, and packet loss.

To understand why speed has become a strategy in itself, we must first recognise a deeper principle at play: *information is only valuable to the extent that it is exclusive and actionable.* In the early decades of financial markets, information asymmetry existed because of geographic barriers, reporting delays, and institutional access. A well-positioned analyst or fund manager could leverage a piece of insight before it became common knowledge, extracting value from the time lag. But with the advent of electronic markets and, later, high-speed data infrastructures, those temporal gaps narrowed dramatically. Today, the edge lies not in *having* information, but in *acting on it faster than anyone else.*

This dynamic has transformed the very structure of markets. Firms like Virtu Financial, Citadel Securities, and Jump Trading invest heavily in infrastructure not for analysis, but for speed. They place servers adjacent to exchange matching engines. They lease dark fibre lines to shave microseconds off transmission times. They build microwave towers between Chicago and New York to circumvent the latency of fibre optics. These are not metaphorical advantages; they are real, measurable, and monetisable. A firm that can execute a trade five milliseconds faster than its competitors can front-run price changes, arbitrage spreads, and react to order flow in ways that are functionally invisible to human participants.

It's important to be clear: this is not "cheating" in any conventional sense. It is competition—taken to its logical, if extreme, endpoint. Regulators have scrutinised the impact of HFT, particularly in the aftermath of events like the 2010 Flash Crash, but the fundamental principle remains intact: *when all other variables are equal, time is the final differentiator.*

What this means for traditional strategic thinking is unsettling. Much of classical investing is premised on the belief that superior reasoning leads to superior results. This assumption becomes fragile in a context where outcomes are driven not by who thought best, but by who acted fastest. It reorients the value chain away from thoughtful positioning and toward technological capacity. Speed, in this context, is not merely a utility—it is a weapon.

Yet the consequences are more than tactical—they are philosophical. When speed becomes the strategy, the *time horizon* of the market itself compresses. Decisions that once played out over quarters or years are now reduced to statistical behaviours over seconds or minutes. The market ceases to be a discursive forum of competing narratives and becomes a dynamic system of continuous optimisation. Liquidity is no longer provided by human market makers but by bots competing for order flow rebates and marginal spreads. The very act of "investing" in this context looks less like analysis and more like engineering.

This shift has also created distortions—both structural and psychological. Structurally, high-speed strategies can lead to *liquidity mirages*: apparent depth that vanishes under stress. Because many HFT firms operate on razor-thin margins, they are extremely sensitive to volatility and tend to withdraw during periods of uncertainty, exacerbating market stress. Psychologically, the emphasis on speed can create a culture of *reaction over reflection.* Traders—both institutional and retail—may feel compelled to act quickly rather than thoughtfully, misreading speed as urgency rather than capacity.

At a deeper level, the elevation of speed raises questions about fairness and accessibility. The infrastructure arms race between HFT firms requires capital expenditures well beyond the reach of most market participants. This creates a tiered system in which those with superior technological access operate in a different version of the market—one where the rules are not different in law, but radically different in effect. Retail traders, for instance, may see a quoted price on their screen that has already been acted upon and changed by faster systems. They are playing a game whose terms they only partially perceive.

One response to this is to treat HFT as a niche—relevant only to specific strategies or asset classes. But this would be a misreading of the broader trend. The ethos of speed has seeped into every layer of the investment stack. Real-time analytics, streaming data feeds, predictive sentiment tools—these are now standard features in institutional toolkits. Portfolio managers increasingly rely on dashboards that update continuously. Risk is recalculated intraday. News is parsed algorithmically before it even hits public wires. Even fundamental analysts now use machine learning tools to process earnings transcripts, track supply chains, and monitor alternative data in near real time.

This creates a subtle, but critical, tension. While *long-term investing* still exists—and in many cases remains the only viable path to structural wealth-building—it now coexists with a system optimised for instantaneity. Strategic patience must now operate within a tactical ecosystem that rewards rapid reflexes. The danger is not that long-term thinking disappears, but that it becomes difficult to maintain in an environment that structurally incentivises short-term action.

So how should thoughtful investors respond?

The answer is not to imitate HFT or chase technological sophistication for its own sake. Most investors cannot, and should not, try to compete on latency. But they must understand how the logic of speed shapes the markets they operate in. That means recognising when price action is driven by flow rather than fundamentals. It means understanding how microstructure affects liquidity, volatility, and order execution. And it means designing strategies that are robust not only to informational uncertainty, but to temporal volatility—the risk that the window to act will close before the analysis is complete.

One emerging approach is the use of *human-in-the-loop systems*—frameworks in which machines do the sensing and proposing, but humans do the approving and contextualising. In this model, speed is harnessed without ceding control. Algorithms flag anomalies or opportunities; humans decide what they mean. This preserves strategic agency while leveraging technological capacity. Another is the use of *bounded automation*, where systems are pre-programmed with specific thresholds and principles but are prevented from executing outside a defined ethical or strategic perimeter. In both cases, the goal is not to compete on speed per se, but to *build systems that remain strategic under time pressure.*

A deeper response, however, is intellectual. Investors must reframe what it means to think clearly in markets saturated with speed. Clarity is no longer just about insight—it is about architecture. How decisions are structured, how information is filtered, and how execution protocols are designed matters as much as the insight itself. Thoughtful investing now requires an operational fluency that includes data latency, execution pathways, and system integrity. To be strategic is not to be slow—it is to be *deliberate within constraint.*

Speed will continue to shape the outer shell of markets. But it is the interior logic—the thinking behind the infrastructure—that determines who stays relevant. The challenge for the modern investor is not simply to move faster, but to *think at the right level of resolution*: fast enough to remain functional, slow enough to remain reflective.

When speed becomes strategy, the playing field changes. But the game is not lost. It simply demands new forms of intelligence—not reactive, not romantic, but rigorously designed. Thoughtful investing is still possible. But it must now occur in a world that does not wait.

# Chapter 2
# What AI Sees That You Don't

For as long as markets have existed, advantage has belonged to those attuned to the undercurrents—those capable of discerning meaning where others saw only noise. Sometimes it hinged on sharper timing; other times, on a more instinctive grasp of collective mood, or simply the foresight to ask the question no one else had yet considered. Historically, the investor's edge was a product of human attributes: patience, interpretive skill, and that curious amalgam of intuition and experience. But today, that edge has begun to shift. It is no longer solely human. A colder, faster, fundamentally alien form of cognition has entered the arena. Artificial intelligence isn't merely enhancing our ability to know—it is reshaping what it means to perceive.

These systems aren't just executing tasks more quickly. They are detecting forms, patterns, and causality in ways human minds weren't built to comprehend. They don't hesitate. They don't agonise. And unlike us, they have no psychological skin in the game. What we're witnessing isn't simply automation for convenience—it's a seismic shift in the underlying mechanisms of cognition. Markets, increasingly, are sculpted not by human thought, but by non-human inference—systems that function without emotion, without understanding, and perhaps even without "thought" as we know it.

Let's begin where the transformation is most apparent: in the machinery of pattern recognition. Humans have always prided themselves on spotting patterns. It's how we survive, how we narrativise the world around us. Yet our pattern recognition comes at a cost—we rely on memory prone to error, heuristics built from limited experience, and emotions that often obscure rather than clarify. AI, particularly in its more sophisticated deep learning forms, operates on an entirely different level. It doesn't seek meaning in the traditional sense; it identifies statistically significant relationships across countless dimensions simultaneously. These models don't need to grasp what GDP is, or why it matters. They simply register how shifts in the data intersect with market movements—and they act.

This isn't theoretical. Firms like Renaissance Technologies, Bridgewater Associates, and Two Sigma are already well down this road. Their systems sift through torrents of data, not to forecast in a narrative sense, but to continually recalibrate their statistical assumptions. From a distance, the process can look almost mystical. But from within, it's ruthlessly mechanical—an extension of computing power applied to the infinitely unpredictable terrain of human economic behaviour.

Yet the truly radical shift is not just how data is processed—it's where that data comes from. The emergence of so-called "alternative data" signals a deep change in what counts as information in the investment world. Gone are the days when quarterly earnings and analyst calls were sufficient. Today's models are parsing satellite imagery, weather patterns, transactional metadata, and geospatial movement. Natural language processors scour transcripts and earnings calls not for content, but for cadence, tone, and veiled sentiment. Where human analysts would be overwhelmed, these systems thrive—sifting signal from a sea of ambient noise.

Consider, for a moment, the implications. A hedge fund adjusts exposure not based on an analyst's report but on footfall trends across shopping centres. Or a reallocation occurs after a language model detects a subtle tonal shift in the regional press of a developing nation. These aren't predictions in the old sense. They're reflexive adaptations to a perpetually shifting informational landscape—interpretations, of a sort, but not the kind a human would easily recognise.

And then there is execution. Machines act with a kind of serene, instantaneous certainty. When the numbers align, they move—without dithering, without regret, without the long shadow of past losses clouding judgement. In a world where milliseconds can define a trade's outcome, that absence of hesitation is more than useful—it's transformative. Human delay, born of introspection or fear, is no longer merely inefficient; it is a structural liability.

Yet—and here lies the rub—machines don't truly understand. They lack the narrative instinct, the sense of context that allows humans to extrapolate meaning in ambiguity. They don't know why something matters; they only know that it correlates. When the world shifts dramatically off-script—during pandemics, geopolitical upheavals, or black swan events—AI systems, for all their speed and scope, often struggle. Not because their maths is wrong, but because their frame of reference doesn't stretch to accommodate the unknowable.

We saw this most starkly during the early months of the COVID-19 crisis. Models, trained on stable economic environments, floundered in the face of cascading, chaotic data. The markets began behaving in ways that no algorithm had ever seen. And in that moment, oddly enough, human investors—those notoriously flawed creatures—often adjusted more deftly. They could improvise meaning without precedent. They could say, "This moment is exceptional," and take action without a model to validate the move.

Which brings us to a crucial juncture: the real divide isn't between human and machine, but between those who know how to collaborate with these systems, and those who don't. It's not a contest. It's a convergence. AI will, without question, dominate in areas requiring speed, volume, and pattern extraction. But human judgement still holds its ground—especially in moments where ambiguity, nuance, or ethical stakes come into play. The task ahead is not to outpace the machines, but to work alongside them with fluency and discretion.

This calls for a new kind of investor literacy—one not grounded in classical fundamentals alone, but in an understanding of models themselves. One must now grasp how algorithms are built, what assumptions they carry, and where their blind spots lie. This is no longer the domain of technical specialists alone. Anyone seeking to navigate modern markets must be conversant in the epistemology of machines.

It's a subtle skill: knowing when a model's conclusion is likely reliable, and when its elegance conceals a fundamental misunderstanding. Not every pattern is meaningful. Not every correlation implies causation. And in some cases, the model may be precisely wrong—brilliantly wrong—because it has mistaken the signal for the story.

That's the tension this chapter sets out to explore. We will examine what machines can see—relationships too complex or fast-moving for human minds to grasp—and how that alters the investment landscape. We'll trace the expanding universe of alternative data and its implications for market logic. We'll delve into the eerie precision of machine execution, and how it distorts human psychology. And then, we'll return to the edges—those areas where machines struggle, where interpretation still requires something closer to human intuition.

If the preceding chapters dismantled the myth of the all-knowing investor, what follows is a mapping of the terrain now emerging. A landscape where cognition is hybrid, where human and machine perspectives interlace and sometimes conflict. This isn't about ceding control. It's about refining our role within a system that no longer resembles the one we trained for.

Because the truth is: the signals are already there. The question is no longer whether you can read them. It's whether you even know what you're looking at.

And with that, let us begin.

## Pattern Recognition Beyond Human Limits

If markets are patterns disguised as chaos, then investing is the act of uncovering order faster and more precisely than others. For centuries, this process has been constrained by the limits of human cognition: what we can observe, interpret, and remember. Even the most gifted traders, analysts, and quants are bounded by the architecture of the human brain—its remarkable intuitions, yes, but also its blind spots. Now, that ceiling is being punctured by systems that operate without those limits. Artificial intelligence, especially in its most advanced learning forms, is detecting patterns so complex, so multi-dimensional, that they are not only invisible to human analysts—they are fundamentally *inaccessible* to the human mind.

This shift is not about speed alone. It is about *depth*—how deeply we can see into the data and how abstractly we can reason from it. In traditional investing, pattern recognition typically meant identifying recurring behaviours in price movements, economic cycles, or behavioural responses. Momentum traders look for trends. Technical analysts search for formations. Value investors detect misalignments between intrinsic and market value. These approaches rely on the brain's intuitive pattern-matching capabilities, honed over time. But no matter how seasoned the practitioner, those patterns are usually shallow in dimensionality: time, price, volume, and perhaps a few correlated indicators.

By contrast, machine learning models can ingest thousands of features—price, volatility, macroeconomic indicators, alternative data streams, news sentiment, supply chain disruptions, social media signals—and model them not as linear associations, but as entangled relationships. A neural network doesn't "see" a market in two dimensions; it models it as a multi-layered structure where every variable potentially interacts with every other in nonlinear ways. This is not just a matter of quantity; it's a qualitatively different way of perceiving the system.

To understand why this matters, consider how a convolutional neural network (CNN) or a transformer-based model is trained. These architectures are designed to learn *latent features*—attributes not explicitly coded by humans, but derived from the internal structure of the data itself. For example, in image recognition, a CNN might detect the curve of a cheek or the edge of a shadow without being told what a face is. In finance, a similar model might learn that a subtle interplay between shipping data, Chinese steel production, and weather anomalies in Brazil has predictive power for iron ore prices. There is no pre-written rule to uncover this. The model simply learns it because it exists.

One of the most striking examples of this in practice comes from the work of firms like Renaissance Technologies, where proprietary models detect statistical patterns so sensitive and fragile that they cannot be fully articulated even by their creators. These patterns may only be exploitable for short periods, under specific market regimes, and may be composed of signals that have no economic "narrative" at all. What matters is not *why* the pattern exists, but *that* it exists—and that it can be acted upon with precision and consistency.

This shift to non-narrative reasoning challenges a core tenet of traditional investing: the explanatory model. Human investors typically want to understand *why* a trade works. They look for justifications—undervalued earnings, shifting consumer behaviour, fiscal policy moves. But AI systems are not constrained by narrative logic. They are indifferent to explanation. If a high-dimensional cluster of data points consistently correlates with asset price movements, the model will act, even if the rationale is incomprehensible to a human observer. In this sense, machines are post-explanatory agents—they *act on patterns* rather than *interpret events.*

That said, this capacity is not without risk. When humans can't interpret a model's output, it becomes harder to evaluate its validity, robustness, or failure points. This is known in the field as the "black box" problem. If a deep learning system tells a portfolio manager to reduce exposure to European equities based on a pattern it can't explain, should the manager comply? Trusting the model without understanding its reasoning introduces operational and ethical risks. Yet rejecting the model simply because it defies explanation may forgo genuine alpha. This epistemic tension—between performance and interpretability—is central to the adoption of AI in finance.

The tension becomes even more acute when models behave adaptively. Reinforcement learning systems, for instance, don't just detect patterns—they learn policies for action over time. These agents experiment, reward themselves based on success metrics, and continually evolve their strategy. In a market context, this might mean dynamically adjusting allocations based on continuously shifting reward signals, including volatility clusters, cross-asset flows, or institutional liquidity imbalances. Such systems are not merely recognising the past—they are *navigating uncertainty* in real time, shaping their strategy with a level of agility no human trader can match.

Importantly, these models are not biased in the same ways humans are. They do not suffer from confirmation bias, recency bias, or overconfidence—unless those distortions are embedded in the training data itself. When trained properly, they can avoid many of the heuristics that cause human investors to misread patterns. At the same time, their objectivity makes them susceptible to *overfitting*—finding spurious patterns that don't generalise outside the sample data. This is particularly dangerous in finance, where regimes shift, correlations break, and historical stability is never guaranteed.

We must also acknowledge that AI's capacity for pattern recognition is a product of its *contextual ignorance*. The same strength that allows it to detect correlations without prejudice also blinds it to semantics. A model may learn that tweets containing certain keywords precede volatility in energy markets, but it cannot evaluate the truthfulness of the underlying statements. It can detect tone, but not motive; sentiment, but not meaning. It is epistemologically blind to irony, propaganda, or political nuance. For this reason, human oversight remains indispensable—not because we can compete with the pattern recognition of AI, but because we provide a form of *judgement* that machines fundamentally lack.

Still, the implications of this new pattern logic are hard to overstate. We are entering a world in which much of the informational alpha has already been harvested before most investors even realise a pattern exists. The speed and dimensionality of machine learning systems mean that *most inefficiencies are arbitraged away at the point of discovery*. The marginal value of traditional research—of reading reports, interviewing management, or charting trends—has been structurally diminished in many market segments. The question is no longer: "What is the pattern?" but "What is the machine seeing that I cannot—and how should that change my approach?"

To operate effectively in this new environment, investors must adopt a dual literacy. They must learn enough about machine learning to understand its assumptions, capabilities, and failure modes. But they must also retain a distinctly human scepticism—aware that not all patterns are meaningful, that not all correlations imply causation, and that even the most precise model is only as good as the logic that governs its deployment.

Pattern recognition beyond human limits is not science fiction. It is already here, embedded in the models shaping fund flows, calibrating risk, and executing trades across the globe. The challenge is not whether we can match the machines—we cannot. The challenge is whether we can *design, interpret, and govern* them in ways that serve our broader investment goals. In this sense, the new edge is not technical. It is philosophical.

Machines see what we can't. The future belongs to those who know how to listen to what they're seeing—and know when to intervene.

## The Quiet Revolution of Alternative Data

Most investors still default to familiar tools: earnings reports, balance sheets, GDP releases, inflation prints, and perhaps a Bloomberg terminal flashing real-time prices. These sources are the established currency of financial analysis—audited, standardised, institutionalised. Yet, while many market participants remain tethered to these conventional data streams, a silent transformation is underway—one that is fundamentally altering how information is gathered, processed, and acted upon. This is the quiet revolution of alternative data.

Alternative data, by definition, refers to non-traditional information sources that were not originally designed for investment decision-making but have become integral to it. Think of satellite imagery tracking the number of cars in retail parking lots. Natural language processing models scanning social media for shifts in consumer sentiment. Geolocation data from mobile phones revealing patterns in foot traffic or migration. Corporate supply chain networks inferred from shipping manifests, patent filings, or job postings. These data types do not replace fundamentals—they *augment and often outperform* them by offering granular, real-time, behaviour-based insights into market dynamics.

This shift is not speculative or fringe. It is happening at the core of how many institutional investors operate today. Hedge funds like Point72, Bridgewater Associates, and QuantCube use alternative data not as a curiosity, but as a key pillar of their research architecture. According to a recent survey by the Alternative Investment Management Association, more than 80% of hedge funds are actively integrating non-traditional data into their investment processes. This is not a trend—it is a regime change.

What makes alternative data revolutionary is not just its novelty, but its *proximity to real behaviour*. Traditional financial data tends to be lagging and sanitised—delivered on a delay, summarised in quarterly intervals, and filtered through regulatory frameworks. By contrast, alternative data captures activity as it happens. A surge in construction site noise detected by audio sensors can precede a spike in industrial output. A decline in real-time restaurant bookings, measured via API from booking platforms, may indicate a localised consumer slowdown before it shows up in earnings reports. These examples are not theoretical. They are used, traded on, and monetised today.

Take the satellite surveillance of oil storage tanks, for instance. By analysing the length and orientation of shadows cast by floating-roof oil tanks, firms like Orbital Insight can estimate inventory levels in real time, even when official data is withheld or delayed. Traders equipped with such insights can position themselves ahead of market-moving releases from the US Energy Information Administration or OPEC. Or consider the rise of web scraping for ecommerce pricing trends—monitoring SKU-level product shifts across platforms like Amazon or Alibaba. This allows investors to track inflation indicators far in advance of national statistical agencies, often with greater specificity.

Another seismic development is sentiment analysis. Natural language processing, once a tool of academia, now sits at the heart of many investment strategies. Models trained on millions of financial news articles, earnings call transcripts, regulatory filings, and even Reddit forums or TikTok captions can extract linguistic cues that signal shifts in market mood or corporate positioning. It's not just about *what* is being said, but *how* it is being said. Is a CEO more confident this quarter? Is a policymaker subtly changing rhetorical stance? Machines can now detect these tonal inflections with remarkable precision.

Importantly, alternative data is not merely additive—it often challenges core assumptions embedded in conventional thinking. For example, traditional economic indicators may suggest that consumer sentiment is stable, while aggregated credit card transaction data reveals a sharp decline in discretionary spending across key regions. Which signal should the investor trust? In many cases, alternative data provides a timelier and more accurate read on underlying conditions, forcing a re-evaluation of what counts as "true" information in markets.

Yet with this power comes critical complexity. The sheer volume, variety, and velocity of alternative data require robust infrastructure and rigorous methodology. Raw data is not insight. It must be cleaned, contextualised, normalised, and—most importantly—*interpreted.* Misreading noise as signal can be costly. A rise in location pings at a retail store may not indicate stronger sales if the store is offering free Wi-Fi that draws loiterers. A drop in hiring activity may reflect automation, not contraction. Understanding the nuance behind the data is not optional; it is essential.

Furthermore, the ethical and regulatory dimensions of alternative data are still evolving. Questions around privacy, consent, and transparency loom large. Should hedge funds be able to trade based on anonymised health data, scraped from poorly secured fitness apps? Should geolocation data be commoditised when most users are unaware their movements are being tracked, sold, and analysed for arbitrage? These are not abstract concerns—they are live debates shaping the boundaries of what is considered acceptable in a surveillance-rich financial ecosystem.

Critically, access to high-quality alternative data is not equal. Many of the most potent data sets are expensive, exclusive, and often negotiated through private partnerships. This raises concerns about information asymmetry in an already unequal market landscape. Retail investors, small funds, and even mid-tier institutions may be structurally disadvantaged—not because they lack intelligence, but because they lack access to the infrastructure that underpins this new informational edge.

Nevertheless, the direction of travel is clear. As computational capacity grows and data acquisition becomes more ubiquitous, the distinction between traditional and alternative data will continue to blur. Eventually, all data will be judged not by its category, but by its *predictive utility*. The frameworks for evaluating investment opportunities will shift from static models to dynamic systems—systems designed not only to incorporate new information but to actively *seek and reinterpret* it in real time.

To operate in this environment, investors must develop a new kind of literacy. Not just fluency in financial statements, but fluency in data provenance, model validation, and contextual interpretation. They must ask sharper questions: What is the source of this signal? What assumptions underpin its collection? How stable is the relationship it purports to represent? Can it be gamed? Is it ethical to use?

The quiet revolution of alternative data is not about replacing human judgement. It is about enhancing that judgement with tools that extend our perceptual range and temporal reach. It is about being willing to see the market not just as a reflection of reported metrics, but as a living, breathing system whose signals are increasingly found in places traditional finance never thought to look.

What matters now is not who has the most experience reading spreadsheets. It's who is willing to listen to the world with new sensors—and who can ask the right questions when those sensors return something unexpected.

The future of investing will belong to those who can integrate these unconventional signals into coherent, adaptive strategies. Not just faster or more technically, but more thoughtfully. With judgement, with clarity, and with a recognition that information itself is no longer what it once was. It is everywhere—and the real skill lies in knowing which signals to trust, and when.

## Emotionless Decisions, Flawless Speed

Markets punish hesitation. In volatile conditions, milliseconds separate profit from loss, precision from noise. While human investors deliberate, machines execute. Not because they're smarter in any intuitive sense, but because they're unburdened. Unburdened by doubt, ego, fatigue, greed, fear, regret. The very qualities that make us human are liabilities in financial systems designed for unforgiving efficiency. Artificial intelligence, when properly designed, acts with an indifference that would be pathological in a person—but is strategic in a machine. *Emotionless decision-making is not just a technical feature; it is an investment edge.*

This edge becomes clearest when viewed through the lens of cognitive bias. Daniel Kahneman's *Thinking, Fast and Slow* permanently altered how we understand decision-making under uncertainty. Humans, as he demonstrated, are consistently irrational in predictable ways. We overestimate rare risks and underestimate compounding effects. We fear losses more than we value equivalent gains. We anchor on irrelevant figures. We follow the herd. These are not minor imperfections; they are systematic distortions that skew judgement across every level of investment activity—from amateur traders panic-selling during a downturn, to seasoned professionals sticking with a flawed model out of sunk cost fallacy.

AI, in contrast, makes decisions without any of these distortions. It does not experience stress under market volatility. It does not second-guess itself. It does not wait to see if others will act first. Once a machine-learning model has been trained and validated, its execution is automatic, reactive only to updated input—not to inner conflict. It acts without the psychological latency that defines human behaviour. In the context of financial decision-making, this emotionless precision is not cold—it's efficient. *AI reduces the decision loop to input, computation, and action.*

This is particularly visible in high-frequency trading environments. A typical HFT algorithm might execute thousands of trades a second, adjusting its positions dynamically based on minuscule shifts in order book depth, arbitrage gaps, or short-term volatility bursts. These decisions happen faster than a human can blink—because no deliberation is required. No emotional friction. No hesitation. And importantly, no false confidence rooted in gut feel. The system is only as certain as its data and model configuration permit. It neither trusts nor doubts; it calculates.

Of course, this doesn't mean AI is flawless. Far from it. Models can overfit, misinterpret noise as signal, or break down when exposed to previously unseen market regimes. But even here, the absence of emotional attachment becomes a strength. Human investors often cling to models or strategies long after they've stopped working—out of identity, legacy, or fear of admitting error. A well-designed machine-learning system will discard its prior beliefs as soon as the data stops supporting them. Its loyalty is to the objective function, not the ego of its creator.

This points to a more subtle and significant benefit of emotionless systems: *they allow us to observe our own flaws more clearly*. By externalising the decision process, AI becomes a kind of diagnostic mirror for human cognition. If a model consistently outperforms a human trader on volatility management, risk parity allocation, or loss minimisation, it's not necessarily because the model is smarter. It may simply be less *conflicted*. The very act of comparing machine outputs to human decisions can reveal where our biases are most corrosive.

This has led to an important evolution in behavioural finance: the development of decision-support systems that *correct for human bias in real time*. Portfolio construction tools can now alert investors when their asset allocations deviate from statistically optimal diversification. Risk dashboards can flag when an investor's position sizing reflects loss aversion rather than logic. Sentiment analysis engines can prompt caution when social media exuberance distorts valuation signals. These are not full replacements for human judgement—but they are *instruments of cognitive hygiene*, helping strip emotion out of processes where it does the most damage.

That said, the relationship between emotionless machines and emotional humans is more nuanced than simple replacement. There are scenarios in which emotional sensitivity is not a flaw, but a feature. During black swan events—pandemics, geopolitical shocks, major regulatory changes—human intuition can sometimes outperform automated models that have been trained only on "normal" market regimes. When the future stops resembling the past, data-driven systems can misfire, because their assumptions collapse. In those moments, the human ability to reframe, reinterpret, and override becomes indispensable.

This underscores the importance of *human-machine collaboration*, not competition. AI should not be seen as an all-knowing oracle, but as a non-anxious partner in an environment that is, by its nature, anxiety-inducing. Machines can manage execution, filter noise, and provide probabilistic clarity. Humans can provide ethical oversight, contextual interpretation, and strategic redirection. In practice, this means structuring decision-making processes that give AI systems autonomy where precision is paramount—and human discretion where ambiguity is unavoidable.

There are already promising examples of this hybrid model at work. Several hedge funds now operate with layered decision frameworks: machine-learning models generate signals based on high-dimensional pattern recognition, while human analysts review those signals for interpretability and contextual relevance. Portfolio managers can approve, reject, or adjust recommendations based on broader macro narratives, regulatory constraints, or ESG considerations. This does not slow the system down; it strengthens it by making it *adaptive rather than rigid.* Emotion is not eliminated—it is disciplined.

Another application is in managing *the emotional load* of investment teams. By delegating high-pressure, time-sensitive decisions to machines, human actors are freed to focus on deeper strategic thinking—less reactive, more reflective. The emotional bandwidth previously consumed by trading adrenaline, confirmation anxiety, or second-guessing can be redirected toward long-term vision and portfolio resilience. Ironically, emotionless execution can *humanise* the investment process by removing the conditions that trigger our worst cognitive instincts.

There is a final, often-overlooked dimension to this discussion: *the ethics of emotionless decision-making.* In financial markets, this tends to be framed as a practical benefit. But in broader societal contexts—credit scoring, insurance underwriting, algorithmic policing—the detachment of AI from human emotion can become problematic. A model that executes flawlessly, but lacks empathy, can make decisions that are technically optimal but morally questionable. This should serve as a caution for financial systems as well. AI should never be granted the authority to make decisions *without oversight or recourse*. Emotionless does not mean value-neutral. Machines must still be aligned with human priorities, values, and principles—even when those are hard to code.

What, then, is the core insight? *Emotionless decision-making is not an endgame—it's a capability*. The real challenge is how we integrate that capability into systems that preserve human judgement, correct human bias, and adapt to uncertainty without being paralysed by it. In finance, where emotion can distort performance and cloud logic, AI offers a form of decision hygiene that is both elegant and indispensable. But the goal is not to remove humans from the loop—it is to elevate their role within it.

Machines execute with clarity. Humans interpret with meaning. The future of intelligent investing depends on how well we reconcile the two—not by choosing one over the other, but by designing systems where *emotionless speed enhances human wisdom* rather than replacing it.

Emotion, in investing, is the source of both our worst mistakes and our best insights. What AI offers is not an erasure of that tension, but a new framework for navigating it—with discipline, precision, and, paradoxically, greater self-awareness.

## Limitations of the Algorithmic Lens

Artificial intelligence, for all its power, does not *understand* the world. It detects, predicts, classifies, and optimises—but it does not *comprehend*. This distinction is more than semantic. It defines the boundary between what AI is good at and where it routinely fails. Investors entranced by the extraordinary pattern recognition and decision speed of algorithms must confront a less glamorous, but equally essential truth: *the algorithmic lens is sharp, but narrow*. It excels at mapping correlations and extrapolating trends, but it falters in the face of context, ambiguity, ethics, and structural surprise.

One of the most persistent misunderstandings about AI in finance is the assumption that because models are data-driven, they must be objective. In reality, models inherit the worldview embedded in their training data. They assume that the future will resemble the past, that market behaviour can be reduced to features, and that risk can be quantified as a function of volatility or drawdown. But financial markets are not closed systems. They are dynamic, reflexive, and shaped by human psychology, regulatory shifts, geopolitical shocks, and collective narratives. No model, however sophisticated, can fully anticipate a system that is *endogenously unstable.*

Consider the problem of context. AI systems are famously poor at understanding anything that isn't in the data. They cannot infer causal logic beyond their statistical associations, nor can they interpret information with cultural, political, or historical nuance. For example, a machine learning model might identify a sharp decline in factory output in a specific region and classify it as a bearish signal for industrial equities. But what if the decline is due to a national mourning holiday, a public health mandate, or a political protest? Without the broader socio-political context, the model can't distinguish between signal and noise—it will treat the anomaly as meaningful simply because it deviates from baseline behaviour.

This inability to parse context is not a minor limitation—it is structural. Unlike humans, who use intuition and world knowledge to infer meaning, machines rely entirely on patterns present in their inputs. If the relevant context was not encoded during training, the model has no interpretive fallback. This becomes especially problematic in emerging markets or in sectors where informal institutions matter as much as formal ones. A strike at a South African mine, a corruption scandal in a Southeast Asian government, or a sudden regulatory pivot in Indian fintech—these are not just data points; they are socio-political events with unique implications that often defy algorithmic classification.

The second major blind spot lies in moral and strategic reasoning. Algorithms are not ethical agents. They can be programmed to optimise for ESG scores, sustainability metrics, or compliance thresholds, but they do not *understand* the ethical trade-offs they are executing. A model may allocate capital away from companies with high carbon footprints, but it cannot evaluate the long-term social impact of doing so on workers, communities, or innovation pipelines. It can score governance frameworks but not *interrogate* their integrity. It can screen for diversity metrics without any understanding of how power dynamics actually function in an organisation.

This limitation becomes especially relevant in fields like impact investing, where the objective is not just financial return but measurable social good. An algorithm can rank microfinance institutions by repayment rates and lending growth, but it cannot ask whether those institutions are empowering borrowers or exploiting them. It cannot evaluate dignity, trust, or empowerment—qualities that resist quantification but are central to many investment philosophies. Ethical investing, by definition, involves subjective judgement, moral framing, and cultural interpretation—domains where human cognition remains indispensable.

Then there is the problem of *unknown unknowns*—the so-called black swans. AI systems, like all statistical models, are inherently backward-looking. They learn from historical data, identify stable patterns, and optimise based on probabilistic distributions. But black swan events, by definition, fall outside the parameters of expectation. They are outliers, discontinuities, structural breaks. The 2008 financial crisis, the 2011 Fukushima disaster, the 2016 Brexit vote, the 2020 COVID-19 pandemic—none of these were predicted by mainstream models, and most were either misclassified or ignored by automated systems in their early phases.

This is not because the data was insufficient. It's because *the assumptions underlying the models collapsed.* Volatility regimes shifted, correlations reversed, market microstructures fractured. And yet, many algorithmic systems continued to operate as though nothing had changed—because, technically, the data still looked "normal" within the bounds of prior learning. The risk here is not merely model underperformance; it is systemic fragility. When too many actors rely on similar models, trained on similar data, making similar decisions, *diversity of thought collapses.* This herding effect can exacerbate crises rather than contain them.

Even in more routine scenarios, algorithmic convergence can erode the informational diversity that makes markets function. When AI systems across firms identify and act on the same statistical patterns, arbitrage opportunities disappear faster, and crowding becomes more likely. What begins as efficiency ends in *homogeneity*, where differentiated thinking is replaced by automated consensus. This is not just a risk for investors—it's a threat to market health. Markets thrive on the tension between differing views, time horizons, and frameworks. A market saturated with identical machine logic becomes brittle.

So how should investors respond to these limitations?

First, by recognising that AI is not a decision-maker—it is a *decision-support tool.* It should be treated as an input into a broader judgement process, not as a substitute for that process. Human oversight should not be a formality; it must be an active, reflective practice. Investors must ask: What assumptions are embedded in this model? What data was excluded, and why? What are the failure modes? What is the model optimising for—and what might it be neglecting?

Second, by building *robustness into system design.* This means stress-testing models across outlier scenarios, diversifying model architectures, and maintaining the human capacity to override automated decisions. It also means integrating interpretability into model development. Tools like SHAP (SHapley Additive exPlanations) and LIME (Local Interpretable Model-agnostic Explanations) allow analysts to understand how models weigh different features—making it easier to detect when the system is relying on spurious signals or overfitting.

Third, by developing *contextual literacy*. Investors cannot afford to be data-blind or model-dependent. They must stay attuned to geopolitical shifts, social movements, cultural currents, and institutional changes that fall outside the scope of most algorithmic systems. Context matters. And it often arrives in forms that cannot be captured in a CSV file.

Ultimately, the goal is not to discredit AI or retreat into intuition. It is to evolve a form of investment practice that recognises both the strengths and the limitations of algorithmic thinking. A practice that combines computational precision with human insight. That respects data but honours meaning. That embraces automation without surrendering discernment.

The algorithmic lens is powerful, but it is partial. It sees the world through the language of patterns and probabilities—but not of ethics, narratives, or institutional nuance. To rely on it exclusively is to risk strategic blindness. But to ignore it is to forfeit a profound edge.

The future of intelligent investing lies not in choosing between human and machine intelligence, but in *designing their collaboration with rigour, scepticism, and care.* Only then can we build systems that are not just faster or smarter, but wiser.

# Chapter 3
# Human Intelligence Reimagined

We've long measured intelligence by its speed, its capacity for recall, and the accuracy of its decisions. By such standards, humans have quietly ceded the high ground. Machines now surpass us in processing power, execution velocity, and their almost eerie ability to extract patterns from data that might drown a human mind. Yet, this creeping dominance of artificial intelligence in finance doesn't relegate human investors to irrelevance. Rather, it calls for a sterner reckoning—a need to reassess not just what we know, but how we know. The edge isn't about being first to the data anymore. It lies with those who choose to think differently, not faster. While AI rushes forward on rails of optimisation, the wisest human investors will step laterally, perhaps even backwards, to redraw the playing field altogether.

This chapter is a meditation on what endures—what remains distinctly human—as finance becomes increasingly algorithmic. Its thesis is both subtle and pointed: the advantage ahead is not technical but philosophical. It's not in sharper analysis or speedier trades, but in the ability to think *about* thinking, to question the frame, to redraw the lines of meaning and purpose. AI may excel at mapping the known, but it cannot reimagine the map itself. The investor of tomorrow will not be the one most fluent in machine logic, but the one courageous enough to reframe that logic altogether.

Let's begin with metacognition—thinking about thought itself. Not just having thoughts, but watching them, questioning them, steering them. This is no idle abstraction; it's one of the few capabilities AI has yet to mimic, let alone master. A neural network can process reams of information and spot arcane patterns. But it cannot stop to wonder whether it's solving the problem that matters. It cannot ask whether the values it serves are worth serving. Only the human mind can reflect on its assumptions, pivot when anomalies surface, tolerate ambiguity, and revise its compass when the landscape shifts.

Philosophical? Certainly. But also the bedrock of strategic clarity in volatile markets.

Consider the moments when the known crumbles. When historical precedent offers no anchor, and when data itself begins to distort. Crises—true ruptures—aren't solved with more precision; they require different perspectives. During the 2008 financial collapse, it wasn't the most elegantly engineered model that saved portfolios—it was the capacity to realise that models themselves had misjudged the nature of risk. Or in the early chaos of 2020, when the pandemic turned the world inside out, the investors who adapted fastest were those who could operate beyond the confines of historical data. Not better machines, but more agile minds.

Behaviour, too, deserves our attention. One might assume that in a world dominated by unemotional machines, human emotion is sidelined. Not so. The emotional quirks of human investors don't vanish—they become magnified. They show up as exploitable inefficiencies, laid bare against a backdrop of machine consistency. When you hesitate out of fear, when you cling to a failed position because of past investment—these aren't just human failings; they're strategic liabilities. And they're going up against systems that never flinch.

This isn't hypothetical. Many investment firms now incorporate behavioural analytics into their decision-making infrastructure. Beyond tracking performance, they're auditing *how* decisions are made. Who tends to become overly cautious after a loss? Who doubles down out of misplaced confidence? These are cognitive fingerprints. And, critically, they can be re-engineered—not just with better habits, but with intentional design. Think pre-commitment checklists, scenario rehearsals, AI-guided nudges. Behaviour can be disciplined, but it can also be redesigned.

And what of ethics? Not as a decorative afterthought, but as a fundamental axis of competence. Machines can optimise, yes—but they cannot care. They don't possess values; they merely pursue the objectives we code into them. That leaves a central burden—and opportunity—squarely on human shoulders. Finance shapes the world: where capital flows, what gets built, who gets access, what gets neglected. Whether you're underwriting a coal mine or investing in green infrastructure, you are making a judgement. Machines might help model the outcomes of those decisions—but they will never tell you which one ought to prevail.

This isn't a failure of AI. It's a reminder. Efficiency is not wisdom. Precision is not discernment. If we want financial systems that serve human ends, we must first define those ends ourselves. It's not about whether AI aligns with human values—it's whether we've done the work of articulating those values with clarity and conviction.

Which brings us to a final, vital shift: the transformation from analyst to architect. Today, much of what passes for strategy is little more than automated reaction. A trigger here, a trade there—a system primed to respond, not to lead. But the most resilient and visionary investors are not responders. They are designers. They construct frameworks rooted not in yesterday's returns but in first principles. They don't wait for markets to define relevance—they define it themselves.

To operate as an architect is to lead with clarity of belief. What is value? What does risk mean—beyond its statistical mask? How do you engage with uncertainty when the models offer no guidance? These are not spreadsheet questions. They're questions of identity, of purpose, of intellectual integrity. They require solitude as much as collaboration. And they resist tidy answers.

So, no—the human investor hasn't become obsolete. But the job has changed. From data-gatherer to system-builder. From pattern-seeker to meaning-maker. The traits once seen as ornamental—ethical judgement, reflective thought, the capacity to sit with uncertainty—are now essential. This is not a eulogy for intuition, nor a lament for a bygone age. It is a manifesto for a deeper, more deliberate intelligence.

Artificial intelligence will continue its steady advance, refining decisions, revealing patterns, stripping away latency. But it will not ask the first question, nor the final one. That work remains ours. And those who embrace that responsibility—who think with rigour, act with conscience, and design with care—they will not merely navigate this new world. They will define its shape.

## The New Human Edge: Meta-Cognition

It is easy to mistake intelligence for speed. In a world dominated by machine learning models that parse billions of data points in milliseconds, the temptation to define superiority by velocity alone is pervasive. Yet, intelligence—*true intelligence*—is not merely the ability to process information quickly. It is the ability to *think about thinking*, to question assumptions, revise mental models, and strategically shift one's lens in light of change or contradiction. This capacity, known as *meta-cognition*, is not only the essence of human adaptability—it is fast becoming the last frontier of human advantage in a financial world run by machines.

The rise of artificial intelligence has redefined what it means to be smart. Algorithms can now detect subtle, multidimensional market signals that no individual could perceive unaided. They outperform humans in pattern recognition, probabilistic modelling, and short-term decision execution. But these abilities, remarkable as they are, remain fundamentally narrow. They are bounded by the rules of their architecture, the scope of their training data, and the incentives defined by their designers. What they lack is the ability to *reframe*. They cannot ask: *Are we solving the right problem? Are we defining risk too narrowly? Is our model still valid in this regime?* Human intelligence, by contrast, can move between levels of analysis. It can step outside the frame and *redesign the logic itself.*

This is meta-cognition: the ability to observe one's cognitive process, detect flaws or rigidity in it, and intentionally alter it. In investing, this capacity has always mattered, but it is now emerging as a critical differentiator. When everyone has access to data and high-performance tools, the edge no longer lies in raw information—it lies in how one constructs meaning from that information. It lies in asking questions that algorithms cannot formulate.

Consider the 2007–2008 financial crisis. The models were sophisticated. The data pipelines were robust. The rating agencies, traders, and quants relied on layers of risk assessment tools calibrated to historical performance. But the problem was not a lack of data or speed—it was a failure of perspective. The models didn't question their own assumptions: that housing prices would not fall nationwide, that correlation among defaults was negligible, that systemic interdependence was manageable. These assumptions were not errors in code; they were flaws in framing. What was needed wasn't more computing power—it was the human capacity to *doubt the foundation.*

Meta-cognition is especially crucial under conditions of volatility and regime change. In stable environments, learned models tend to perform well. But in markets shaped by geopolitical rupture, pandemics, demographic realignment, or ecological constraint, the ability to *re-evaluate one's premise* becomes far more important than the ability to optimise within a model. AI, in such contexts, tends to become brittle. Human meta-cognition, though slower, becomes more adaptive.

This is not a theoretical distinction. Meta-cognitive investors—those who regularly reflect on their decision-making processes—are often better at handling uncertainty. They develop habits of stepping back: Why did I make that trade? What assumptions was I relying on? What did I ignore or underweight? They incorporate feedback loops not just to adjust parameters, but to question whether the framework itself needs restructuring. Over time, this kind of thinking creates not only resilience, but genuine strategic foresight.

Psychological research supports this. Studies in decision science and behavioural economics have shown that individuals who exhibit high levels of meta-cognitive awareness tend to perform better in dynamic and complex environments. They are less susceptible to overconfidence, better at recognising noise, and more skilled at distinguishing between correlation and causation. These traits are not innate. They are cultivated—through practices such as reflective journaling, post-mortem analysis, and deliberate model revision.

In the investment world, however, these practices remain rare. The industry still rewards decisiveness over reflection, confidence over doubt, and short-term results over long-term process improvement. But as algorithmic decision-making becomes ubiquitous, the comparative value of human intuition and improvisation diminishes—unless it is coupled with *intentional abstraction.* That is, unless it's used not to compete with machines, but to do what they fundamentally cannot: *reconceptualise the game.*

Let us take a concrete example. Suppose a machine learning system is trained to identify undervalued equities based on price-to-earnings ratios, earnings momentum, and sector rotation. It performs well during a bull market cycle. But then the macroeconomic environment shifts—say, due to central bank policy, climate regulation, or political upheaval. The model, trained on historical data, starts to fail. A non-meta-cognitive investor might tweak the inputs or switch models. A meta-cognitive investor, by contrast, asks: *Why did this work in the first place? What assumption am I carrying about the relationship between valuation metrics and future price movement? Is the very premise of mean reversion still valid in this environment?*

This kind of thinking doesn't always yield immediate results. It requires cognitive effort, a tolerance for ambiguity, and often, the courage to act against consensus. But over time, it builds a much deeper form of intelligence—one that can adapt across regimes rather than optimise within them. And in financial markets, regime shifts are not exceptions; they are the rule.

Meta-cognition also has ethical implications. Investors who reflect on their thinking are more likely to reflect on their *impact.* They ask not only what returns they are generating, but what consequences they are enabling. They consider the systemic effects of their strategies—on labour markets, ecological systems, social trust. These are not secondary considerations. In a world of interconnected risk, ethics is not a moral luxury—it is a form of strategic awareness. Algorithms can be trained to screen for ESG factors, but only humans can ask whether those factors are meaningful, or merely a proxy for reputational management.

Importantly, meta-cognition can be taught. It is not an abstract trait reserved for philosophers or seasoned strategists. It is a practice, a discipline, a set of routines. Organisations that institutionalise reflective practice—through decision audits, structured feedback, open intellectual culture—often outperform those that rely on instinct or brute force. Investment firms that create space for deliberate reasoning, even in the face of market urgency, are not slowing down—they are *building capacity for better decisions.*

The challenge, of course, is that meta-cognition does not scale easily. It is time-consuming, introspective, and often uncomfortable. It reveals bias, exposes blind spots, and invites humility. These are not qualities traditionally celebrated on trading floors or in quarterly reports. But they are exactly what is needed in a world where markets are increasingly complex, narratives are fragmented, and technology amplifies both insight and error at unprecedented speed.

The future of investing will not belong to those who react fastest. It will belong to those who *think in layers*—who can shift between systems-level understanding and granular detail, who can interrogate their own reasoning while engaging the market, who can move beyond prediction to reflection. As AI continues to extend its dominance in the realm of speed, scale, and precision, the most valuable human skill will be our ability to *stand above the machine, not race against it.*

Meta-cognition, then, is not a luxury. It is not an optional add-on for the philosophically inclined. It is the foundation of a truly modern investing mind. It is what allows human intelligence to remain relevant—not by mimicking machine logic, but by thinking *beyond* it. It is the discipline that transforms data into insight, action into understanding, and investment into a form of *designed thinking.*

And in this, the human investor does not merely survive the age of AI. They redefine its meaning.

## Behavioural Investing in the Age of Bots

The great paradox of modern investing is that while machines have become more rational, humans have not. As algorithms increasingly dominate financial markets—executing trades with flawless logic, at speeds that elude human comprehension—the spotlight turns not to competing with these machines, but to understanding what remains uniquely human. And that begins with the mind. Specifically, it begins with the biases, heuristics, and emotional triggers that shape investor behaviour—often subconsciously, yet decisively.

Behavioural finance, once a niche field on the fringe of economic orthodoxy, has become indispensable in an AI-mediated landscape. Where once investors operated in markets largely shaped by human judgment, today they navigate ecosystems increasingly governed by non-sentient actors. These actors—algorithmic trading systems, robo-advisors, machine learning platforms—do not succumb to fear, greed, or loss aversion. They do not panic in a downturn or chase exuberant rallies. They do not anchor, overreact, or fall prey to confirmation bias. In short, they *do not behave.* They execute.

This introduces a profound shift in the strategic mindset required of human investors. In markets where many players no longer possess emotions or psychology, the relevance of behavioural insight doesn't diminish—it *amplifies.* Because if the machines are no longer irrational, the residual irrationality belongs almost exclusively to the humans. And recognising this is the first step toward investing with clarity, rather than illusion.

Consider the anchoring effect—a well-documented cognitive bias wherein individuals rely too heavily on the first piece of information they encounter. In pre-AI markets, when most participants were human, this might have created herd-like behaviour: if a company's stock dropped significantly from a previous high, investors might view it as a bargain, regardless of whether fundamentals had deteriorated. But in a machine-dominated environment, such psychological "bargains" often fail to rebound as expected—because the bots aren't emotionally tethered to past price levels. They react to signals, not sentiment.

Or take the disposition effect: the tendency to sell winners too early and hold onto losers too long. Human investors, driven by loss aversion and the desire to "be right," frequently sabotage their returns by exiting profitable positions prematurely while waiting for underperformers to recover. Algorithms, however, operate under no such compulsion. Their sell signals are based on statistical thresholds and risk parameters—not the psychological relief of "locking in a gain" or the pride of not admitting defeat. When trading alongside such entities, human weakness becomes glaring. And costly.

This raises an uncomfortable but necessary question: *Are we willing to hold a mirror up to our own biases, now that the market no longer shares them with us?*

The answer determines whether human investors remain relevant in a digital financial landscape. Because the truth is, behavioural biases were somewhat concealed when markets were dominated by other equally flawed humans. Collective irrationality could cancel itself out. Mispricings were abundant. Sentiment cycles moved predictably from fear to greed and back again. Traders could read the mood of the market as if reading a room.

But today, much of the room is filled with actors that don't have moods. Algorithms don't chase trends—they anticipate or create them. They don't interpret macro headlines emotionally—they model them probabilistically. They don't fear missing out—they are never "in" emotionally to begin with. This changes the behavioural game. It forces human investors to be more self-aware, because the old psychological signals are now largely one-sided.

This is not merely a call for emotional discipline. It is a call for *cognitive literacy*. It requires knowing not just that you are biased—but *which* biases you are prone to, *when* they tend to surface, and *how* they interact with market structure and machine logic. A trader who knows they tend to become risk-seeking after losses may decide to automate position sizing to remove discretion. An investor prone to confirmation bias may deliberately build a "red team" process into their research workflow—tasking themselves to argue against their own thesis before acting. These are not merely good habits. They are essential counterweights to deeply wired vulnerabilities that machines can now systematically exploit.

And that exploitation is real. Quant firms have learned to model and profit from predictable human errors. High-frequency trading strategies are designed to detect and arbitrage behavioural tells: panic selling, overreaction to earnings surprises, or volume spikes that signal herd behaviour. Even large institutional investors are not immune; their rebalancing patterns, order sizes, and flow timing can be reverse-engineered and anticipated by sophisticated algorithms. What was once merely human weakness is now monetisable *alpha*—for the machines.

So where does this leave the reflective investor?

Ironically, in a position of advantage—*if* they are willing to evolve. The emergence of AI in investing does not render behavioural insight obsolete. It makes it more vital than ever. But the focus must shift. It is no longer about predicting market sentiment as a collective human mood—it is about managing *personal cognitive risk* in an environment that increasingly lacks it elsewhere. This requires a toolbox that includes introspection, cognitive science, and behavioural design.

Practical steps matter. Journaling trades and the reasoning behind them—not just the outcomes—can help identify emotional triggers and recurring patterns. Developing structured pre-mortems ("How might this trade fail?") creates space for disconfirming evidence.

Instituting cooling-off periods before large investment decisions, or using checklists to remove impulsivity, can add layers of discipline that blunt the edge of emotional reactivity. These techniques are not glamorous. They do not require machine learning. But they embody *behavioural sophistication*, which is now as critical as financial acumen.

There is also a deeper strategic shift underway: one that repositions human behaviour not as a liability, but as a terrain of opportunity. While machines can detect and exploit behavioural patterns, they cannot *understand* them in a meaningful sense. They cannot intuit intention, infer moral nuance, or redesign incentive structures. They cannot judge the reliability of a CEO's off-script comment, or the ethical ambiguity of a corporate action. These are interpretive acts, rooted in human insight. And they matter.

Moreover, the future of markets will increasingly be shaped not just by data, but by *narratives*. Machines can scan sentiment, but they cannot contextualise stories. They can measure frequency of words, but not the *gravity* of ideas. The role of the human investor, then, is not to outcompute the bots—but to *outframe* them. To understand that behaviour is not just bias—it is *contextual intelligence*. And when aligned with ethical judgment and reflective practice, it becomes a competitive edge.

This is where behavioural investing must go next. It cannot be confined to identifying irrational anomalies in others. It must be retooled as a form of *self-governance* in a post-human trading environment. It must become less reactive, more reflective; less about emotion suppression, more about *cognitive architecture*. The investor who can design their own decision-making environment—who can intentionally craft the context in which their biases are triggered or constrained—will outperform the one who simply tries to will their way to discipline.

Because the machines don't feel. But they can sense when we do. And if we are unaware of our own psychology, we're playing against a silent opponent who knows our playbook better than we do.

To thrive in this new terrain, we need to stop mimicking machines. We must start *mastering ourselves*. That is the real work of behavioural investing today. Not avoiding all emotion—but cultivating an intelligent relationship to it. Not pretending to be flawless—but designing for our flaws. Not racing the bots—but thinking differently from them.

In the end, the advantage is not in being faster, or even smarter in the computational sense. It is in being *conscious*. And that begins with one question: *What part of my investing behaviour is mine—and what part is simply a reflex waiting to be hacked?*

Only those who dare to ask—and answer—that question will remain meaningfully human in a world that no longer requires them to be.

## Ethical Judgment as a Differentiator

Among the many myths circulating in modern finance, one of the most persistent is that markets are morally neutral. Numbers are presumed to be objective, returns agnostic, and algorithms immune to values. But beneath every investment lies a set of assumptions—about time, about risk, about worth. These are not just technical constructs; they are ethical choices, whether consciously made or passively inherited. In an age where algorithms dominate the mechanics of investment, *ethical judgment remains one of the few distinctly human advantages*. And unlike speed or scale, it cannot be replicated by machine logic.

To understand why this matters, we must start by examining the limitations of AI—not in terms of processing power, but in terms of purpose. Machine learning systems are designed to optimise. They identify patterns in data, predict likely outcomes, and choose actions based on pre-defined reward functions. In trading, this typically means maximising return within given risk constraints. But *what defines return?* What qualifies as risk? How do you weigh long-term systemic harm against short-term gain? These are not questions machines can answer. They require value judgements—and value judgements require ethics.

Consider a real-world example. An AI system managing a large equity portfolio might identify that a certain mining company is undervalued relative to its historical cash flow metrics. It may also detect that political instability in the region is subsiding, making the company a candidate for rebound investment. However, that same company may be embroiled in controversies over environmental degradation and displacement of local communities. The algorithm, absent any ethical input, will prioritise the return signal. But a human investor must decide whether profiting from that rebound aligns with their principles. The machine optimises for what *is*. The human decides what *ought* to matter.

This becomes especially consequential when we move from individual investments to institutional scale. Pension funds, sovereign wealth funds, and endowments increasingly manage capital that affects millions of lives. The inclusion—or exclusion—of weapons manufacturers, fossil fuel producers, or companies with poor labour practices is not a matter of market mechanics. It is a matter of long-term consequence. And these decisions cannot be outsourced to optimisation engines, because they depend on factors that are *not quantifiable*: fairness, dignity, ecological stewardship, intergenerational justice.

Ethical investing is not new. What is new is the pressure to make it operational in a world where AI excels at narrow optimisation but fails at broad discernment. Environmental, Social, and Governance (ESG) frameworks attempt to bridge this gap, but they often do so through metrics that strip nuance from complex issues. A company may score well on environmental criteria for reducing emissions, while simultaneously engaging in aggressive tax avoidance or exploitative supply chain practices. A machine can tally scores. But only a human can *interpret them in context.*

This is where ethical judgment becomes strategic, not just moral. Investors who can engage in ethical reasoning—who can assess trade-offs, foresee reputational risks, and anticipate the evolving expectations of society—are not just doing the right thing. They are often making the *smart* decision. Public tolerance for externalised costs—whether environmental, social, or governance-related—is diminishing. Regulation is tightening. Stakeholder scrutiny is intensifying. Companies that ignore these forces may deliver short-term profits but face long-term erosion. Ethical investors are not taking a principled detour from market logic; they are expanding the logic to include *all the variables that actually shape outcomes*.

Yet the practice of ethical judgment in investing is difficult, in part because it resists codification. There is no universal algorithm for moral reasoning. Values vary across cultures, contexts, and timeframes. What seems defensible today may appear negligent tomorrow. Investors must therefore learn to operate in ambiguity—to weigh competing goods, to question simplistic trade-offs, to think in terms of *consequence* rather than *compliance*. This is not an act of moral purity. It is an act of *disciplined reflection*—of taking responsibility for the systems one's capital sustains.

There is a growing body of research from behavioural ethics and moral psychology that reinforces this need. Studies show that ethical blind spots often arise not from malice, but from mental compartmentalisation. When financial actors view their role as separate from social or environmental impact, they become more likely to tolerate or ignore harm. Conversely, when they are trained to consider broader stakeholder implications, they make more holistic—and often more resilient—decisions. This is not soft science. It is a competitive advantage rooted in self-awareness.

It is also, crucially, human. Algorithms may eventually be trained to simulate ethical decision-making, perhaps by learning from past case studies or encoded organisational principles. But this remains mimicry, not understanding. Machines do not experience shame, empathy, or moral regret. They do not reflect. They do not wrestle with ambiguity. They do not ask whether their success is built on someone else's suffering. They optimise, but they do not *contemplate.* And in investing—as in leadership—*contemplation matters.*

We are now entering a period where the ethical dimension of capital allocation is being called into sharper focus. Whether it's AI's role in surveillance capitalism, the environmental cost of digital infrastructure, or the labour conditions behind supply chains, the boundaries of what is considered "material" are expanding. Investors can no longer plead ignorance. Nor can they defer to machines. The judgment calls that define the future will be made not at the level of execution, but at the level of *intention.* What kind of world are we financing? What behaviours are we rewarding? What trade-offs are we willing to accept—and which ones should we reject outright?

This is not about virtue signalling or moral superiority. It is about taking seriously the fact that finance shapes society. When human judgment is absent from that process, the system becomes mechanical, unaccountable, and—ultimately—fragile. When ethical judgment is present, it becomes adaptive, self-correcting, and trustworthy. And trust, especially in a world of increasing algorithmic opacity, is the foundation on which enduring investment performance is built.

In this subchapter, we will explore how ethical reasoning can be made actionable within investment decision-making. We'll examine historical case studies where ethical foresight outperformed short-term gain. We'll look at contemporary frameworks for integrating values into portfolio construction. And we'll analyse how investors can cultivate ethical literacy—not as an abstract ideal, but as a *pragmatic skill set* for thriving in a world where the boundaries between markets, technology, and morality are rapidly collapsing.

The age of AI in investing is not just a technological transition. It is a philosophical one. And as machines take over more of the "how," humans must increasingly take responsibility for the "why." Ethics is not a soft constraint on hard logic—it is the *deep structure* of meaningful investment. Machines can calculate return. Only we can define value.

## From Analyst to Architect

For decades, the archetype of the investor has been rooted in the analyst: the person who responds to information, interprets patterns, calculates risk, and reacts strategically. This figure—armed with spreadsheets, earnings reports, and economic forecasts—was defined by responsiveness. Their skill lay in processing available data more effectively than their peers, extracting actionable insights, and placing bets with speed and precision. But as artificial intelligence assumes the role of supreme analyst—processing signals at speeds and volumes no human can match—the value of reaction is being fundamentally redefined. The era of the analyst is giving way to something else. Something more rare, more human, and more consequential: the architect.

What does it mean to become an investment architect? At its core, it means shifting from tactical reaction to strategic creation. Architects are not faster calculators or superior pattern recognisers; they are framers of systems, designers of mental models, and curators of long-term priorities. While the analyst asks, *What is the data telling me today?*, the architect asks, *What kind of investor do I intend to be over the next twenty years—and what structure best supports that vision?*

This shift is not merely stylistic. It's existential. As machine learning continues to dominate the tactical plane—reading market signals, parsing news sentiment, adjusting to volatility in microseconds—the human edge must be redefined around the one skill machines do not possess: *philosophical intentionality*. Machines do not design goals. They optimise toward objectives given to them. Humans alone can choose what *should* matter. And that choice, more than any trade or allocation, is what defines strategic sophistication in this new landscape.

Let us begin with the practical limitations of remaining in the reactive mindset. In an investment world saturated with predictive algorithms and real-time data analytics, being the first to know is no longer a meaningful advantage. The latency gap between information surfacing and market reaction has collapsed to milliseconds. By the time a human sees a headline or a trend, AI-powered traders have already priced it in, moved the capital, and recalibrated. The responsive investor, once considered sharp and adaptive, is now at perpetual risk of being a day late and a basis point short.

Yet even as speed becomes meaningless, the pressure to chase it remains. Many investors, institutional and individual alike, still cling to behavioural scripts forged in the twentieth century—watching news feeds, adjusting positions daily, looking for arbitrage opportunities in crowded, AI-dominated spaces. The result is a hollow mimicry of relevance. Instead of shaping markets or insights, many are simply echoing signals already processed more efficiently by machines. The problem is not that they're irrational. It's that they're obsolete.

Contrast this with the architectural mindset. Architects step back from the daily noise and build investment systems aligned with enduring values, durable insights, and evolving life contexts. They select tools not because they're popular, but because they fit the structure they are consciously designing. They craft portfolios around goals—not only financial but also ethical, psychological, and intergenerational. They spend less time reacting to market noise and more time refining the *purpose* and *philosophy* of their participation in the financial system.

One of the most powerful expressions of the architectural mindset is the integration of *meta-decisions*—not just choices within markets, but choices about how one engages with markets at all. For example:

Do you automate certain allocations to reduce emotional volatility? Do you delegate tactical rebalancing to a robo-advisor while retaining strategic oversight? Do you invest in public equities for liquidity and private ventures for impact? Each of these is a design decision. And unlike reactions to a headline or earnings report, design decisions accumulate into a coherent worldview.

This coherence is not easy to achieve. It requires the investor to examine their own assumptions, clarify their values, and build a system robust enough to function under uncertainty but flexible enough to evolve. It demands philosophical depth, psychological insight, and a refusal to be swept along by the tyranny of the immediate. In this way, the architect is not a passive allocator of capital, but an active curator of meaning.

This reframing has major implications for how we think about investor education, advice, and responsibility. Traditional investment education has focused on interpreting financial statements, understanding economic cycles, or mastering valuation models. These skills are not irrelevant, but they are no longer differentiators. A more future-facing curriculum would include systems thinking, cognitive bias training, ethical decision-making, and scenario planning. The next generation of investors must learn not just how to analyse, but how to *architect.*

Consider a parallel from the world of medicine. For much of history, doctors were trained diagnosticians. Their prestige came from their ability to assess symptoms, recall conditions, and prescribe treatment. But as diagnostic tools became more advanced—first with imaging, then with genetic data, and now with AI-assisted analysis—the doctor's unique role shifted from interpretation to *judgement.* Machines can identify anomalies, but only humans can weigh trade-offs, values, and patient contexts. In investing, the same shift is underway. Data is now abundant, but meaning is scarce. Analysts decipher. Architects decide.

This also reshapes the relationship between humans and AI in investment contexts. The real power of AI is not that it replaces the investor, but that it frees the investor to focus on higher-order thinking. Instead of chasing signals, the architect delegates the legwork to machines and reclaims the cognitive space needed for deliberation. When AI becomes a subordinate tool, not a competing intelligence, it unlocks the freedom to reflect, design, and lead. The investor becomes less like a chess player and more like the rule-maker of the game.

That said, architectural thinking also introduces new responsibilities. It requires confronting the ethical implications of one's financial actions—not just what earns the most, but what builds the world one wants to inhabit. Are your investments aligned with environmental sustainability? With social justice? With long-term community resilience? These are not questions AI can answer. They are fundamentally human inquiries, demanding human engagement. The architectural investor must take seriously the moral architecture of their portfolio, not just its numerical return.

Moreover, architects must embrace a more dynamic conception of identity. They are not fixed in their strategies or doctrines. They continuously revise their structures in light of new knowledge, shifting priorities, and evolving macro conditions. This is where the real artistry lies—not in getting it "right" once, but in building an adaptable scaffold for perpetual learning and reconfiguration. As investor Howard Marks has famously written, "You can't predict. You can prepare." Preparation, in this context, means design.

So how does one begin this transition from analyst to architect? The path starts with reflection. What are your core investment beliefs? How did you arrive at them? Which are still serving you, and which are holdovers from outdated contexts? Next comes intentional design: What time horizons truly matter to you? What risks are you willing to live with? What values must your capital express? From there, build systems that support, rather than sabotage, these aims—

automations that reduce noise, advisors who challenge your blind spots, tools that clarify rather than confuse.

The future of investing will belong to those who can think structurally, act deliberately, and adapt creatively. The analyst will always have a role—but increasingly, that role will be operational, not strategic. The architect, by contrast, remains essential. Because no matter how fast machines become, they will never have a sense of purpose. And in a financial system flooded with data, *purpose is the final edge.*

The investors who endure—and shape the future—will be those who stop reacting and start building. They will recognise that their portfolios are not just containers of assets, but expressions of ideas. They will understand that capital allocation is a creative act, not merely a technical one. And above all, they will reject the illusion of passivity and embrace their role as intentional designers in a world that desperately needs strategic clarity. They won't just play the game. They'll design the board.

# Chapter 4
# Portfolio by Algorithm: Tools That Think for You

The investor's toolkit has undergone a transformation of quiet but seismic magnitude. The days of the paper ledger, the instinctive hunch, the thumb-worn calculator—they now feel almost quaint. In their place stands an arsenal of hyper-responsive digital platforms, parsing torrents of data at speeds no human could hope to match. Where once a portfolio was crafted with care and time, it is now engineered—often in moments—by tools that don't merely assist but participate, influencing outcomes as much as they help shape them.

This chapter ventures into the heart of that transformation. Not just a tale of tech adoption, but of a deeper handover—an intellectual outsourcing, if you will. Algorithms aren't simply handling execution; increasingly, they are designing the scaffolding of financial thought itself. And that, understandably, unsettles. After all, these systems don't comprehend context. They don't grasp the subtext of social change or the moral nuance of a difficult trade. But what they offer instead is hard to ignore: relentless optimisation.

It's a different world now. Gone are the heuristics and gut calls that once governed allocation. In their place, dynamic systems simulate market shifts in real time, adjusting variables across tax brackets, time horizons, and liquidity preferences with surgical efficiency. Picture a young engineer in Bangalore, looking to grow their wealth steadily over the next few decades. The system assembles a bespoke portfolio—risk-matched, tax-optimised, retirement-conscious—within seconds. Across the globe, a retired teacher in Edinburgh gets the same treatment, calibrated for an entirely different life chapter. The tools don't sleep. They don't forget. And they don't deviate from their programmed pursuit of optimality.

And make no mistake: this is more than mere convenience. It's the convergence of money management and computational design. Once the preserve of elite investment houses, advanced simulations—modelling entire economies or projecting multi-decade outcomes—are now accessible through subscription apps. Democratised, yes. But also depersonalised. What, then, is our relationship to tools that don't just guide, but act?

Robo-advisors have been at the vanguard of this shift. Their rise has mirrored the preferences of a generation raised on frictionless tech and algorithmic logic. Initially, these platforms offered little more than simplified allocation, funnelling users into pre-defined risk profiles. But that was only the beginning. Today, leading systems analyse behavioural tics, optimise withdrawal strategies for tax efficiency, and adapt continuously—not just to markets, but to the ebb and flow of their users' lives. Somewhere along the line, the tools stopped being mere instruments. They became quasi-fiduciaries.

Meanwhile, the frontier has expanded. AI-driven optimisation tools have moved well beyond classical finance theory. No longer confined by Markowitz's clean but narrow paradigms, these models employ reinforcement learning, Bayesian inference, even evolutionary logic. They adapt not only to volatility, but to the unique arc of an investor's story. They detect nonlinearities, uncover hidden risks, and recalibrate without pause. The inputs? Not just market signals, but shipping data, consumer sentiment, even the digital murmurs of social media.

Yet with all this power comes a different sort of vulnerability. These systems, elegant though they may be, are opaque. They can dazzle with their precision—and still be fundamentally misguided. One false correlation, one misread anomaly, and the machine's outputs drift off course. And because the inner workings are often inscrutable, their errors resist explanation. We may sense that something is amiss, but lack the vocabulary—or access—to diagnose it.

Enter the digital financial twin. A near-perfect simulation of you, constructed in software, running lifelike forecasts across decades. It knows your goals, your patterns, your constraints. It tests outcomes across a myriad of "what ifs": a premature retirement, a market crash, a policy change. This isn't speculative fiction. It's already embedded in the workflows of family offices and forward-leaning institutions. It allows for rehearsal before reality—a sort of sandbox for life's big financial decisions.

But step back, and you'll see something larger in motion. The very nature of investing is shifting. Less about prediction, more about configuration. The central question is changing, too. No longer "What's the market going to do?" but "What do I want my system to optimise for?" It's a subtler recalibration, but a profound one. The skills that matter now? Framework-building, not just number-crunching.

Lest there be confusion: this isn't a paean to passivity. Quite the opposite. It's a call for discernment. For all their strengths, machines still lack the one thing only humans possess—the ability to assign meaning. They can process, yes. But they cannot prioritise. They can extrapolate, but not deliberate. They can answer, but only if we're the ones asking the right questions.

And that is the real danger—not that the algorithms will fail, but that we will forget how to think. That we'll grow content with outputs and forget to examine the assumptions they're built upon. That we'll mistake consistency for wisdom. That we'll let go of the steering wheel not because the car drives better on its own, but because we've lost the appetite for driving.

In the pages ahead, we'll navigate this emerging terrain. We'll track the evolution of robo-advisory from blunt tool to behavioural mirror. We'll probe how modern AI isn't just refining optimisation, but reimagining it entirely. We'll peek inside the risk models that promise visibility, yet often operate in shadow. And we'll examine the rise of the digital twin as both model and mirror of our financial selves.

At every turn, the focus won't be solely on what these tools can do—but on how we, as thinking participants, might use them more wisely.

This isn't about surrendering our judgement. It's about sharpening it. Less technician, more architect. Less trader, more strategist. The machines, make no mistake, are extraordinary. They compute faster, more thoroughly, and without fatigue. But they do not care. They do not choose.

That, still, is our privilege. And our burden.

## The Rise of the Robo-Advisor

*From Passive Algorithm to Personalised Architect*

In 2008, as the global financial system convulsed under the weight of its own contradictions, a quiet shift began on the periphery of wealth management—a shift not catalysed by central banks or macroeconomic theory, but by lines of code. That year, amid the ruins of traditional finance, a startup called Betterment launched with a deceptively simple premise: what if investing could be automated—not just in execution, but in judgment? It was the first mainstream robo-advisor, and it didn't simply repackage index funds. It redefined who the investor was and who—or what—should guide them.

Today, robo-advisors manage trillions in assets worldwide. But the story is no longer about convenience or low-cost diversification. It's about intelligent personalisation, predictive modelling, and the accelerating delegation of financial agency to machines. The rise of the robo-advisor marks not the marginal improvement of traditional advisory models, but their philosophical inversion. Where human advisors once built trust through conversation, today's robo-advisors build it through frictionless precision. Where intuition once reigned, probabilistic logic now presides.

This chapter examines how robo-advisors have evolved from rule-based allocators into adaptive financial architects—systems capable not only of managing portfolios, but of shaping the very financial consciousness of their users.

## From Simplified Guidance to Systemic Intelligence

In its early form, the robo-advisor was a rules engine: a platform that asked a few basic questions—"How old are you?", "What is your risk tolerance?", "When do you plan to retire?"—and mapped the responses to a generic asset allocation model. The appeal was cost-efficiency and ease of access, particularly for younger investors priced out of traditional advice.

But as machine learning, behavioural finance, and data integration matured, the architecture of robo-advisors changed. Today's platforms are less about choosing between a handful of ETFs and more about designing dynamic, optimised, tax-efficient, behaviourally adjusted financial plans in real time. They don't just allocate—they adapt. They don't just execute—they infer.

Consider Wealthfront's "Path" or Schwab's "Intelligent Portfolios." These platforms analyse cash flow, savings habits, even spending patterns, to make continuous recommendations. They harvest tax losses at the level of individual securities, predict when you might go over budget, and nudge you gently back into alignment. What we once called "advice" has become embedded system logic—contextual, responsive, and often invisible.

*The implication is profound: personal finance is no longer a sequence of decisions but a system of feedback loops, orchestrated by software.*

## The Psychological Shift: Trusting the Machine

Trust, in finance, was traditionally a human phenomenon. We trusted our advisor because he looked us in the eye, remembered our children's names, and shared our economic worldview. But that model rested on two assumptions: that the human advisor was competent, and that their biases were aligned with our best interests. The former has proven inconsistent; the latter, increasingly untenable.

In contrast, robo-advisors demand a different kind of trust—not interpersonal, but systemic. They ask us to trust the impartiality of algorithms, the statistical validity of models, and the integrity of design. And they do this in a world that remains deeply uncomfortable with algorithmic opacity.

Yet adoption grows. Why? Because the benefits are difficult to ignore. Robo-advisors don't panic. They don't churn portfolios to boost commissions. They don't retire, take holidays, or fall ill. Most importantly, they are engineered to act in line with a defined utility function—whether that's maximising after-tax returns, minimising drawdowns, or optimising for longevity-adjusted income. That makes them, in many cases, more consistent fiduciaries than human advisors ever were.

*The question is no longer whether people trust machines with money—but whether they trust themselves more.*

### Architecting the Portfolio in Real Time

Modern robo-advisors are now edging toward a role once reserved for elite private wealth managers: constructing and adjusting portfolios in real time based on personalised, multidimensional data.

This is not merely a matter of rebalancing a 60/40 split when it drifts. It involves:

**Integrating tax considerations**, such as capital gains harvesting and asset location strategies.

**Adapting to life changes**, such as a job loss, birth of a child, or change in income—all inferred through connected data sources.

**Responding to market volatility**, not with blanket risk-off signals, but with specific, risk-adjusted tilts.

**Simulating economic stress tests**, using historical and synthetic datasets to evaluate portfolio robustness.

Crucially, this sophistication is not limited to the ultra-wealthy. By collapsing operational costs, robo-advisors democratise what was once premium expertise.

Yet sophistication introduces its own risk: *over-delegation.* As investors become increasingly dependent on the outputs of these systems, there is a danger that financial literacy declines just as financial outcomes become more mechanised.

### The Architecture of Choice: Personalisation Without Complexity

One of the most underappreciated achievements of advanced robo-advisors is their ability to manage *complexity invisibly.* Behind the scenes, they may be running multi-objective optimisation algorithms, Monte Carlo simulations, or deep reinforcement learning loops. But the user sees none of this. What they experience is *clarity*—a simple dashboard, a progress bar, a monthly check-in.

This user experience design is not incidental. It is philosophical. Complexity is abstracted not to obscure, but to *empower.* The investor is relieved of computational burden without being infantilised. They are given tools, not tasks.

This changes the relationship between investor and system. Instead of being an operator, the user becomes a *collaborator*—setting preferences, expressing values, and reviewing results, while the machine executes and adapts. In this way, robo-advisors nudge users not toward passivity, but toward a more reflective form of agency.

### Limitations, Vulnerabilities, and Ethical Design

Despite their capabilities, robo-advisors are not oracles. They reflect the priorities of their designers, the constraints of their models, and the boundaries of the data they ingest. Their recommendations are statistical, not moral. Their assumptions are implicit, not debated.

For instance, most robo-advisors optimise for mean-variance efficiency, assuming historical correlations and volatility remain reasonably stable. But black swan events, behavioural herding, or geopolitical shocks can quickly invalidate these assumptions.

Moreover, personalisation has limits. Few platforms meaningfully incorporate *values-based investing* or *long-term societal impact.* Even fewer expose their underlying models to public scrutiny. *Transparency*, therefore, becomes a differentiator—an ethical as well as practical imperative.

There is also the broader question of *autonomy.* At what point does convenience become dependence? If your entire financial worldview is shaped by an interface you didn't design and an algorithm you don't understand, are you still the investor—or merely the beneficiary?

### The Human Role: Oversight, Interpretation, and Meaning

What, then, remains of the human role? The answer is not technical oversight—machines outperform most people in that arena. It is *philosophical governance.* Humans must still ask the questions that machines cannot: What are we optimising for? What trade-offs are acceptable? What does wealth mean beyond utility?

Robo-advisors can forecast cash flow and balance risk, but they cannot define purpose. They can simulate outcomes, but not *ethics.* The investor's job, therefore, is not to out-compute the machine—but to *contextualise its outputs within a broader moral and strategic horizon.*

In the age of algorithmic investing, to be a great investor is no longer to have the best thesis or the fastest trade. It is to know which variables *matter* and to design one's financial life in accordance with values that no spreadsheet can quantify.

## AI-Driven Portfolio Optimisation

*How Intelligent Systems Recalibrate the Rules of Risk, Return, and Time*

Modern investing has long been tethered to a deceptively simple triad: risk, return, and time. The challenge, of course, has never been in recognising these variables—it's in managing the tension between them. For decades, this calculus was handled using models that balanced historical averages, assumed normal distributions, and relied on the investor's ability to stomach volatility. But today, that delicate balancing act is no longer a solitary human endeavour. It is being delegated, recalibrated, and increasingly *reimagined* by machine intelligence.

AI-driven portfolio optimisation represents a decisive shift in how we conceptualise risk, how we pursue returns, and how we align investments with evolving objectives. It's not just about using algorithms to crunch numbers faster. It's about enabling portfolios to *learn*, adapt, and re-optimise in response to signals that no human could process at scale or speed. AI systems are now parsing real-time market data, alternative data, behavioural patterns, and even regime shifts in macroeconomic environments—all to engineer portfolios that remain not just "efficient," but *intelligent.*

This isn't portfolio theory with a software upgrade. It's a philosophical reframing of what it means to optimise financial life in a nonlinear, data-dense, uncertainty-riddled world.

### From Static Allocation to Adaptive Intelligence

The conventional approach to portfolio construction—rooted in Harry Markowitz's Modern Portfolio Theory (MPT)—assumes that investors can build an optimal mix of assets by balancing expected returns against expected volatility. But the model has limitations: it requires stable correlations, predictable asset behaviour, and a relatively fixed risk tolerance. In practice, these assumptions rarely hold.

AI breaks this rigidity by treating portfolio construction as a *dynamic process*, not a static event. Rather than optimise once and rebalance quarterly, modern AI systems assess risk exposures continuously, integrating live data feeds, adjusting for changing market conditions, and—critically—learning from outcomes. This means portfolio weights are no longer tied to backward-looking heuristics but are constantly reshaped by *forward-looking inference.*

For example, an AI optimiser might detect subtle changes in liquidity dynamics across global markets—shifts too minor for a human to notice—and reduce exposure to vulnerable assets hours or even days before a drawdown. It might identify anomalous correlations between commodities and currencies during periods of geopolitical stress, adjusting cross-asset exposure accordingly. In short, *the machine doesn't just follow rules—it rewrites them in response to the environment.*

**Beyond Risk and Return: Multidimensional Utility Functions**

Traditional portfolio models usually optimise for a single objective: risk-adjusted return. AI systems, however, can optimise across *multiple dimensions simultaneously*, reflecting the messy complexity of real-life financial goals. These might include:

Capital preservation during specific life stages

Income generation with tax sensitivity

Exposure to ESG criteria without sacrificing diversification

Drawdown management under stochastic volatility regimes

This is possible because AI does not require elegant equations—it thrives on messy data and imperfect patterns. Techniques such as reinforcement learning, evolutionary algorithms, and neural networks allow optimisers to simulate thousands of paths and infer the best decisions under uncertainty, not certainty.

In practice, this means portfolios are increasingly *bespoke*, not just in asset composition but in their strategic logic. For a 45-year-old entrepreneur with variable income, the optimiser may tilt towards liquidity and low-correlation hedges. For a 30-year-old software engineer with equity compensation, it may incorporate behavioural nudges to reduce concentration risk. These are not recommendations—they are *structural configurations*, baked into the portfolio itself.

### Time Horizons as Variables, Not Constants

One of the most underrated strengths of AI-driven optimisation is its ability to treat *time* as a flexible, contextual variable. Traditional advice often uses fixed brackets—short-, medium-, and long-term horizons—assuming linearity in goals and risk exposure. But real life does not unfold in linear segments. Illness, opportunity, economic shifts, and even sentiment can reconfigure an investor's horizon overnight.

AI platforms can model this uncertainty using probabilistic simulations. For instance, if early retirement becomes feasible due to unexpected windfall or career change, the optimiser can reorient the portfolio structure *without human prompting*, adjusting for longevity risk, withdrawal rates, and inflation expectations in real time.

Importantly, AI systems don't just react to input—they *anticipate transition*. Using historical patterns and behavioural models, they may predict when an investor is likely to increase their risk appetite (e.g., post-debt payoff) or become more conservative (e.g., during caregiving years), enabling pre-emptive adjustment of asset exposures.

*Time, in this framework, is not a fixed input. It is a dynamic parameter that the system learns to understand and adjust for.*

## The Role of Data: Inputs that Redefine Insight

AI-driven optimisation is only as good as the data it ingests—and that data now extends well beyond price histories and economic indicators. Increasingly, optimisation engines are incorporating *alternative data* sources such as:

Social sentiment trends and news velocity

Satellite imagery of retail foot traffic or industrial activity

Real-time spending behaviour and credit utilisation

ESG performance data from supply chain disclosures

Climate risk projections for real asset exposure

The result is not just better forecasts, but *context-aware optimisation.* For example, a portfolio that includes infrastructure equities may adjust for climate volatility based on regional flood risk. A portfolio heavy in consumer discretionary stocks may use anonymised transaction data to detect spending slowdowns ahead of earnings season.

This is not predictive astrology—it's probabilistic inference with materially relevant consequences. The optimiser doesn't make bold claims about "what will happen." It continuously recalibrates probabilities in light of *what is changing*, and adapts accordingly.

## Ethical Considerations and Design Bias

While AI-driven optimisation offers unparalleled sophistication, it is not without concern. The systems still reflect the design priorities—and blind spots—of their creators. Optimisers may inherit biases from training data, prioritise short-term gains over long-term ethics, or amplify systemic risks by reinforcing herd behaviours.

There is also the risk of *hyper-optimisation*: portfolios so finely tuned to recent conditions that they lose resilience in the face of regime shifts. This is why leading-edge platforms now incorporate *robustness constraints*—deliberate underfitting, diversification beyond mathematical efficiency, and periodic injection of randomness to ensure broader tail protection.

Ethically, AI systems should also be transparent about their objective functions. If a robo-advisor is optimising for fee efficiency or proprietary product preference, the user should know. *Algorithmic opacity is not a feature—it's a liability.*

### Reframing the Investor's Role

As portfolios become more autonomous, the investor's role must also evolve. It is no longer enough to assess allocation or check returns. The investor must now act as a *governor of systems*—defining objectives, interrogating assumptions, and choosing when and how to trust machine inference.

The new skill set is *meta-cognitive*: understanding not just markets, but the logic behind the models mediating our exposure to them. Investors must be fluent not in programming languages, but in strategic interpretation. They must ask not only "what is this system doing?" but "what does it believe?" and "is that belief aligned with my values and needs?"

This is not the end of investing. It is the beginning of *design-based investing*—where strategy is not improvised in crisis, but encoded in systems that learn, evolve, and align with human goals through iterative collaboration.

## Risk Models Reprogrammed

*How Machine Learning Is Rewriting the Language of Financial Uncertainty*

Risk, for most of modern investing history, has been a matter of measuring what happened yesterday to infer what might happen tomorrow. From the capital asset pricing model (CAPM) to value-at-risk (VaR), traditional risk models have relied on static equations and historical data to anticipate volatility, price shocks, and worst-case scenarios. But these tools were designed in a world of comparative slowness—where economic trends developed over quarters, not hours, and where market dislocations were the exception, not the expectation.

Today, we no longer inhabit such a world. Markets move at algorithmic speeds, fuelled by real-time data streams, geopolitical complexity, and behavioural feedback loops. Uncertainty is not a tail event—it is a structural condition. In this new environment, static risk models have begun to fail not because they are wrong, but because they are *too slow, too narrow, and too brittle.* Their assumptions—about correlations, distributions, and stationarity—do not hold under stress, precisely when they are needed most.

This is where machine learning enters the frame. AI-driven risk models are not simply faster calculators of old ideas. They represent a fundamental shift in how financial systems *perceive, adapt to, and prepare for* uncertainty. These models do not ask, "What was the volatility last year?" They ask, "What signals suggest that volatility is *changing now*—and why?"

The shift is not just technical. It is philosophical. It reframes risk not as a quantity to be measured, but as a behaviour to be *watched, learned from, and acted upon.* The implications for portfolio design, regulation, and investor psychology are profound—and still unfolding.

**The Fragility of Old Frameworks**

To understand what's being reprogrammed, it helps to revisit what came before. Traditional risk models are built on a bedrock of elegant simplifications. CAPM, for instance, uses a single factor—market beta—to explain asset risk and return. It assumes investors are rational, markets are efficient, and returns are normally distributed.

VaR, one of the most widely used risk measures, attempts to estimate the maximum expected loss over a given time frame, at a given confidence level. But VaR has become infamous for its blind spots. It cannot account for black swan events, it fails under extreme nonlinearity, and it presumes stable relationships in data that are anything but.

The 2008 financial crisis exposed these flaws with devastating clarity. Financial institutions that appeared robust under traditional risk metrics proved dangerously fragile. Models calibrated to years of calm failed catastrophically when confronted with regime shifts and systemic interdependencies they could neither see nor understand.

What these models lacked was *context sensitivity*. They treated risk as a fixed feature of the landscape rather than a living, breathing system capable of changing shape—and doing so without warning.

**Risk as a Dynamic Signal**

Machine learning reverses this limitation by treating risk not as a summary statistic, but as a *signal environment*. Rather than relying on historical averages, AI-based models ingest vast datasets—from tick-level market data to social sentiment, macroeconomic indicators, and even natural language newsfeeds—to generate a constantly updating view of financial risk.

One of the clearest illustrations is the use of recurrent neural networks (RNNs) in volatility forecasting. These models do not assume that tomorrow's volatility will resemble yesterday's. They *learn patterns* across time—detecting structural breaks, cyclical behaviour, and anomalies—and adapt their forecasts accordingly.

Whereas traditional models might require manual intervention to adjust assumptions, AI models *self-correct*. If correlations between asset classes begin to collapse—as they did in March 2020—machine learning systems can detect these shifts in real time and reprioritise hedging strategies or asset allocations without relying on human intuition or slow-moving recalibration protocols.

The speed of response is critical. In many cases, by the time traditional risk metrics begin to flash red, AI models have already begun to pull back exposure or shift to lower-volatility assets.

### Real-World Use: From Quant Funds to Risk Officers

This is not theoretical. Leading quant hedge funds—such as Renaissance Technologies, Two Sigma, and Citadel—have been using machine learning-based risk models for years. Their systems process terabytes of data daily, adjusting exposures across thousands of positions, often invisibly to outside observers.

But the trend is no longer confined to elite trading firms. Institutional asset managers, pension funds, and insurance companies are now incorporating AI-based risk analytics into their core platforms. Risk officers are being asked not only to monitor compliance thresholds but to *interpret machine-generated forecasts* of tail risk, drawdown probability, and liquidity fragility.

Even retail platforms are beginning to integrate machine learning tools into their back-end systems. Robo-advisors use these tools to dynamically adjust client portfolios in response to economic indicators, volatility spikes, or behavioural triggers—such as panic-driven withdrawals.

This marks a profound change in who controls risk and how. The act of risk management is being outsourced not to individual advisors or risk committees, but to systems designed to learn, predict, and act on patterns that human observers could neither detect nor process at scale.

### Are AI Models Inherently Better?

There is a temptation to treat machine learning as a panacea—as if its complexity guarantees superiority. This is dangerous. While AI systems can detect nonlinear relationships, adapt to real-time data, and improve with training, they also introduce new forms of opacity and fragility.

The most advanced models—such as deep learning systems—are often black boxes. They may forecast a rise in tail risk, but cannot always explain *why*. This lack of interpretability makes it difficult for risk managers to validate or override their outputs. It also raises accountability concerns, particularly in regulated financial environments.

Moreover, AI models are vulnerable to *overfitting*—where a system learns noise instead of signal—and *regime dependency*, where patterns learned in one environment fail to generalise in another. During sudden macroeconomic shocks, even the best-trained models may revert to ineffective behaviour if they were calibrated during a period of artificial calm.

That is why the best institutions now combine AI tools with *human-in-the-loop systems*—where human judgement supervises machine outputs and interrogates assumptions. The future of risk management is not man versus machine. It is *machine-augmented human discernment.*

### Redefining Risk Itself

Perhaps the most interesting development is not the evolution of models, but the expansion of what *counts* as risk. AI systems can detect and quantify new forms of vulnerability that traditional models overlook entirely:

**Sentiment risk**: a sudden collapse in investor confidence detectable through natural language processing of social media or news

**Liquidity risk**: an evaporation of bids in asset markets, modelled using real-time order book data

**Climate risk**: projected changes in asset viability based on region-specific climate models

**Contagion risk**: cross-asset shock propagation detectable through network analysis

These are not theoretical constructs. Machine learning models at major investment firms now integrate these indicators into daily assessments. A sudden uptick in negative sentiment toward Chinese equities, a weather anomaly in a crop-producing region, or a change in credit default swaps can all trigger portfolio adjustments *before* prices react.

This redefinition of risk matters. It allows investors to see fragility not just as volatility, but as *structural vulnerability*—across geographies, asset classes, and time horizons.

### A New Vocabulary for a New Reality

What machine learning brings to risk modelling is not just new tools, but a new language. It teaches us that risk is not a static number to be looked up in a table. It is a moving signal to be sensed, interpreted, and responded to—continually, intelligently, and contextually.

We are moving from a world of risk quantification to one of *risk interpretation*. The challenge is no longer to calculate volatility but to understand *how volatility behaves*, and how systems—not just markets, but investor behaviour, geopolitics, and ecological patterns—interact in complex, emergent ways.

The most successful investors of the next decade will not be those who rely on the best spreadsheet or the cleanest data set. They will be those who can *collaborate with intelligent systems*, understanding both their strengths and their blind spots. They will be interpreters of risk—not as technicians, but as strategic thinkers who treat uncertainty not as a flaw in the system, but as its defining feature.

## Your Digital Financial Twin: Simulating Tomorrow to Decide Today

There was a time when financial planning meant sitting across from an adviser, pencil in hand, sketching retirement projections on paper using assumptions so general they bordered on fiction. Income, expenses, a vague estimate of inflation, and an "average" risk appetite were the tools of the trade. But finance no longer resides in such simplifications. Increasingly, it's not only your investments that are being managed by algorithms—it's *you.* Or rather, an AI-generated model of you: your Digital Financial Twin.

This isn't science fiction or a metaphor for a new budgeting app. A Digital Financial Twin is an evolving simulation of your financial life that incorporates real-time data inputs and probabilistic forecasting to map decision outcomes with a level of granularity impossible for traditional methods. It doesn't just show you what might happen if you save more or retire later; it simulates the cascading consequences of those decisions through hundreds of interdependent financial pathways—adjusting dynamically as your actual life unfolds.

This article examines how Digital Financial Twins work, what makes them distinct from prior generations of financial models, and why they represent both a technological leap and a philosophical reframe. We also explore their implications for autonomy, privacy, and the very idea of "financial literacy" in an AI-guided age.

**From Static Spreadsheets to Living Simulations**

Traditional financial models have always relied on deterministic inputs. The investor specifies a goal—say, £1.5 million by age 65—and the software generates a path based on historical averages: expected returns, inflation rates, and withdrawal patterns. These systems are useful, but brittle. They're often blind to life's nonlinearities: career pivots, health shocks, inheritance surprises, market anomalies, and behavioural missteps. They plan for the probable, but not the personal.

The Digital Twin upends this by functioning not as a plan, but as a *parallel self.* It integrates live data from a variety of sources—bank transactions, investment platforms, insurance records, tax filings, even wearables tracking your health—to build a high-fidelity financial model that mirrors your real-world behaviours and evolving life conditions. Where older models treat you as a theoretical investor, the Digital Twin treats you as a *data-emitting organism*, subject to constant change.

Moreover, the simulation is not passive. It runs thousands of stochastic forecasts based on machine learning algorithms that continuously refine assumptions based on macroeconomic inputs (e.g., interest rate shifts, employment trends) and micro-level signals (e.g., how your spending changes seasonally or post-promotion). The result isn't a single trajectory, but a *probability field*—a multidimensional map of potential futures, constantly recalculated.

**The Architecture Behind the Twin**

Under the hood, a Digital Financial Twin relies on three core components:

1. **Data Fusion Engine**: This layer ingests and synchronises inputs from banking APIs, market feeds, tax authorities, employment data, and even digital life signals (e.g., geo-location habits, subscription services). Its job is to normalise and contextualise these disparate streams into a coherent user model.

2. **Behavioural Modelling Framework**: Unlike spreadsheets, which assume consistent behaviour, the twin models financial psychology. Algorithms analyse your transaction patterns to infer risk tolerance, impulse control, and preferences under uncertainty—traits that are often more predictive than income or net worth alone.

3. **Forward Simulation Engine**: The core engine runs Monte Carlo or agent-based simulations under various policy or scenario changes: What if you reallocate 20% of your portfolio to private markets? What if healthcare costs double? What if your company IPOs or you're laid off at 52? These aren't just hypotheticals—they're stress-tested across thousands of simulations with adaptive learning loops that recalibrate over time.

This system doesn't replace decision-making. It reframes it. Rather than asking "What's my number?", users are asked, "Which risk pathways are you prepared to tolerate?" or "Which values do you want your money to express?"

### Philosophical Shift: From Planning to Pattern Recognition

Perhaps the most radical shift introduced by the Digital Twin is how it reframes our relationship to time and agency. Financial planning used to be about *control*—locking in assumptions and plotting a path. The Twin moves us toward *navigation*—surfing a constantly changing topography of opportunity and risk.

This requires a different kind of literacy. Not just understanding APRs or the difference between stocks and bonds, but grasping how systems evolve, how feedback loops amplify or dampen effects, and how apparently minor decisions today can alter the branching structure of your financial future. *It teaches investors to think probabilistically, not deterministically.*

In practice, this means that investors are no longer tasked with "getting the plan right" but with managing *resilience under complexity*. A Digital Twin can tell you which sequences of returns are most dangerous for your retirement, when to de-risk based on early warning signals, or how changing residence affects tax drag across jurisdictions. This isn't prediction; it's *preparation*—at scale and in real-time.

### Use Cases: Practical, Personal, and Institutional

Consider a 35-year-old freelancer in the gig economy. Income is erratic, savings lumpy, and retirement benefits non-existent. A traditional financial adviser might struggle to model this volatility. A Digital Twin, however, can integrate real-time income data, model cashflow volatility, and offer probabilistic forecasts for mortgage eligibility, insurance needs, and retirement sufficiency—all while adjusting for local tax codes and asset class correlations.

Now consider a pension fund. By deploying aggregated Digital Twins for its member base (with privacy preserved), the fund can simulate behavioural risks—like premature withdrawals or shifts in contribution rates—under various macroeconomic shocks. This allows for better hedging strategies, communications targeting, and plan design.

### Ethical Fault Lines: Prediction vs Manipulation

But with power comes ambiguity. When a Digital Twin becomes too accurate—able to predict with precision how you'll spend, save, or panic—where is the line between insight and influence? Could financial platforms nudge you toward "optimal" decisions that serve their commercial interest more than yours?

There's also the problem of *overfitting identity*. If a Digital Twin learns your patterns too well, does it lock you into a probabilistic cage? Human beings are not merely predictable agents; they are aspirational ones. The point of modelling is not just to anticipate behaviour, but to *expand optionality*, to show us who we *could be*, not just who we've been.

Hence, ethical use of Digital Twins must preserve surprise, support deviation, and reinforce autonomy. Transparency in algorithmic design, opt-outs from behavioural profiling, and explainability in decision logic will all be necessary to ensure these systems remain tools—not tyrants.

### The Investor as Co-Designer

What makes the Digital Financial Twin truly revolutionary isn't its computational horsepower—it's the invitation it extends. For the first time, individuals are not just passive users of financial systems, but *co-designers of simulations* that reflect their values, strategies, and evolving identities.

Used wisely, this reframes personal finance as a living dialogue—not a plan you follow, but a system you adapt. You aren't just managing money. You're managing *uncertainty*, *time*, and *identity*—with a machine that's watching, learning, and helping you do it better.

The future of investing may be digital, but it doesn't need to be dehumanised. The Digital Twin, if built responsibly, is not the replacement of human intelligence—it's its augmentation. A mirror not of what we are, but of what we might yet become, when we learn to think ahead of ourselves.

# Chapter 5
# Wealth as an Information System

In the world of capital markets, we've long leaned on a binary logic to define wealth: gains versus losses, growth against contraction, up or down. It's a tidy framework—satisfying, even. But increasingly, it feels ill-suited to the times. The financial reality we now inhabit hums with sensors, algorithms, and layers of semantic processing. Money, once a straightforward vessel for value or exchange, has grown strange. It acts more like information than matter—shifting, signalling, shaping. Every investment becomes a data point, a gesture that ripples across a vast and twitching network. The modern investor, then, isn't simply managing assets—they're managing meaning.

To understand what wealth has become is to grasp how it has turned fluid, computational, and interpretive—an architecture less about static value than evolving context. Price charts and earnings ratios still have their place, certainly. But they're embedded in a broader matrix: of stories, algorithms, heuristics, and inference loops. Think of physics, where energy never disappears but merely alters form. So too with capital—it moves, recycles, reconfigures—but its significance is always in flux. And in this domain, foresight isn't enough. What's required is interpretive dexterity: the ability to sit with ambiguity, to update internal models, to remain composed while logic is handed over to machines.

So let's start with a claim that may sound metaphorical, though it isn't: money is data. Not poetically, but structurally. Capital flows today echo the architecture of information systems. They respond to micro-signals, initiate via code, and adapt in real time to shifts in sentiment and context. Machine learning models don't merely track—they anticipate, probabilistically reading between the lines, often extracting pattern from what appears, to us, as noise. Markets now resemble complex organisms—restless, adaptive, in constant feedback with the informational environments that nourish them.

And if we take this seriously, the implications for how we think about risk, return, and value are significant. Viewed through the lens of thermodynamics, markets begin to resemble open systems—ever increasing in entropy as data floods their boundaries. Chaos theory, often relegated to the edges of science, becomes surprisingly apt. Tiny perturbations—an offhand tweet, a sudden policy shift—can send shockwaves. Yet from that disorder, shapes still emerge. The investor today doesn't just navigate volatility; they swim in a fluid, non-linear information ecology. AI tools attempt to model this chaos, adjusting constantly, but often remind us of a deeper truth: there is no universal map. Only a shifting landscape of probabilities.

Within this constantly reforming terrain lies another tension—an older one, though now newly urgent: the dissonance between story and number. Algorithms optimise outcomes. They tune for yield, for Sharpe ratios, for tax efficiency. But humans crave coherence. Institutional investors pursue ESG mandates or intergenerational stewardship. Individuals back ventures that reflect their ethics, aspirations, or identities. To some, these impulses appear soft, even irrational. Yet that misses the point entirely. Such choices embed narrative in the flow of capital; they bring moral intention to bear on statistical logic. They are ways of saying, "This is what matters"—in a language finance can sometimes forget how to speak.

Must we choose between sentiment and statistics? We argue not. In fact, the most forward-looking investment philosophies now embrace both. Consider how Nordic sovereign funds explicitly integrate long-term equity across generations. Or how certain family offices design around resilience, not just returns—framing portfolios as instruments of stewardship rather than mere gain. These aren't a rejection of quant. They're its deepening. A layering of purpose atop precision. A reintroduction of human scale into a domain increasingly shaped by silicon.

The idea that emerges may seem provocative: that one can—and arguably should—invest in meaning. This isn't a flourish. It's a shift in posture. As AI automates ever more of the procedural heavy lifting, our role as human decision-makers must ascend, not vanish. What matters now is not just asking, "What might this yield?" but "What does this support?" Not only, "Is this efficient?" but "Is this aligned with the future I wish to build?" Our edge may not lie in speed, but in context. In asking better questions. In stepping back long enough to see the system, not just the metric.

What follows in this chapter isn't a technical breakdown of AI in markets—there are enough of those elsewhere. This is a reorientation. A way of looking anew at capital—not as a detached abstraction, but as something embedded in relationships, communities, time. Markets, through this lens, are less like algorithms and more like ecosystems. Messy. Interdependent. Teeming with feedback loops, both seen and unseen. And value? It begins to appear not just in short-term gain, but in resonance, integrity, and enduring relevance.

In this light, wealth becomes something richer than what sits in your account or your balance sheet. It's tied to your understanding of the system you're part of—and what you choose to do with that awareness.

## Reframing Money as Data: How Financial Decisions Became Signals in an Information Economy

The most radical transformation in modern finance isn't blockchain, cryptocurrency, or even AI—it's the reframing of money itself. Not as capital in the traditional sense, but as *data.* In today's algorithmically intermediated world, financial behaviour is increasingly interpreted not through the lens of scarcity or utility, but through information theory. To invest is to transmit a signal. To hold, to sell, to hedge—each decision encodes preference, belief, intent, and probability. And it is precisely this shift—from value as a store of purchasing power to value as interpretable data—that marks a quiet, yet profound, epistemic rupture.

Money, at its core, is no longer simply what we spend or save. It is what we *express.* Algorithms now learn from portfolios the way linguists once studied dialects: to uncover patterns, anticipate movements, and decode motivations. Financial life is becoming legible to machines—not because they understand human meaning in the way we do, but because meaning, when scaled, behaves like data. Predictable, extractable, and—critically—optimisable.

The implications are far-reaching. Portfolio management, macroeconomic modelling, and behavioural forecasting are increasingly driven not by first-order observations but by second-order inferences—what choices imply about the chooser. This is not a semantic game. It is the architecture of modern financial infrastructure.

To grasp what this means, we must revisit the philosophical assumptions baked into traditional finance, and then examine how they unravel when exposed to the logic of machine intelligence.

*The Price Is Never Just the Price*

Classical economic theory is built on a foundational illusion: that price reflects intrinsic value. Markets, in this worldview, function like mirrors, reflecting fundamentals—earnings, assets, competitive advantage—back to a rational investor. But markets are not mirrors. They are conversations. And in that conversation, price is not a conclusion. It's a hypothesis, shaped by human emotion, algorithmic feedback loops, and increasingly, by real-time global data streams.

When money is treated as data, pricing becomes a probabilistic statement rather than a static fact. The value of a stock is not what it's "worth", but what the aggregated information system believes it *might be worth*, conditional on a cascade of evolving variables. This reorients the role of the investor. Rather than discovering value, the investor becomes a signal processor—decoding noise, updating priors, and managing uncertainty.

This reconceptualisation aligns with Claude Shannon's original insight: information is that which reduces uncertainty. When an investor makes a choice—say, to overweight technology stocks—they are producing information in the Shannonian sense. And when hundreds of thousands do so in aggregate, AI systems use those collective signals to update models, assess systemic exposure, and even predict regulatory response. *Every dollar moved becomes a data point in a machine-parseable language of intent.*

*From Asset Allocation to Signal Architecture*

Modern portfolio theory, built by pioneers like Harry Markowitz and William Sharpe, approached investing as an optimisation problem—balancing risk and return across uncorrelated asset classes. Yet these models assumed relative independence, rationality, and stationarity. Today, none of those assumptions hold. Markets are interlinked, dominated by reflexive behaviour, and shaped by dynamically shifting variables.

AI-driven models now treat portfolios less as mathematical compositions and more as information ecosystems. Tools ingest structured data—like earnings reports, volatility indices, and bond spreads—and combine it with unstructured data—tweets, weather patterns, political developments—to create adaptive, self-improving systems. The objective is not only to optimise for Sharpe ratio or volatility drag, but to *learn* from how investors react to new information and reframe what "risk" actually means.

Consider how hedge funds use satellite imagery of retail car parks to estimate revenue projections for consumer goods companies before earnings season. Or how NLP systems scan executive tone during earnings calls for indicators of confidence, deception, or deflection. These are not merely analytics—they are ways of turning *human nuance into machine-readable input.*

This evolution turns investing into a kind of Bayesian reasoning. Every data point is a prior. Every choice updates a belief. In such a model, information is not a supplement to decision-making. It is the substrate of decision-making itself.

*Entropy and the Limits of Predictability*

If money is now data, it must also obey the laws of information theory. That includes entropy—the measure of uncertainty in a system. The more unpredictable a variable, the higher its entropy. In financial markets, entropy manifests as volatility, correlation breakdowns, or black swan events. Traditional models treat these as aberrations. AI-infused systems treat them as *features*.

This distinction is critical. Classical models aim to reduce uncertainty through diversification. But intelligent systems aim to *measure* it, map it, and simulate its effects in advance. AI doesn't eliminate entropy, but it can learn to model its contours. Reinforcement learning agents—akin to those used in game-playing AIs like AlphaGo—simulate possible market paths and adjust strategy based on anticipated reactions to volatility. Risk, in this framework, is not an input but a *consequence*—emergent from the interaction between multiple informational agents, each updating in real-time.

Yet this power has a blind spot. Models are only as robust as the data they ingest. And not all meaning is quantifiable. Some of the most consequential investment decisions are made in response to *narrative*, not numerical input.

### *Narratives as Latent Variables*

There is a quiet tension emerging in the financial world between numerical analysis and interpretive meaning. AI excels at detecting statistical correlation. But it struggles with causation, especially when driven by cultural, psychological, or ethical reasoning. Narratives—stories about inflation, climate risk, geopolitical conflict—don't conform neatly to regression lines. Yet they shape market behaviour more profoundly than balance sheet ratios ever could.

This is where human cognition retains an edge. Investors do not only process data; they *interpret events*. When Elon Musk tweets about Bitcoin, or when a central bank subtly changes its tone, human investors intuit context. Algorithms may quantify the textual change, but they cannot understand it with the same semantic granularity.

This isn't a case for rejecting data. It's a case for integrating it with human narrative intelligence. The most effective investors of the future will not be pure quants or pure storytellers. They will be *narrative-systems thinkers*—those who can read the story, analyse the signal, and reconcile the two without defaulting to either.

*Toward a Philosophy of Financial Meaning*

To treat money as data is not to diminish its importance. Quite the opposite. It elevates money from a medium of exchange to a *carrier of intent.* Every financial decision becomes a message: this is what I believe about the future; this is what I value; this is what I'm willing to risk. The challenge for modern investors is to recognise this shift—and to respond accordingly.

This calls for a new kind of literacy. Not just financial literacy, but *epistemic literacy*—the ability to understand what a piece of data actually represents, what it *doesn't* capture, and how systems will likely react to it. Investors must ask: *What am I signalling by this allocation? What assumptions are embedded in this model? What might this choice mean five years from now, in a world of changed climate, culture, or regulation?*

These are philosophical questions. And they must be asked not despite AI, but *because* of it. As machines grow more powerful in parsing data, humans must grow more adept at interpreting meaning. The edge is no longer access to information. It is the ability to *contextualise it.*

*The Future Is Semantically Aware*

Looking ahead, we will see increasing convergence between semantic AI and financial systems. Natural language models trained on economic history, behavioural finance, and ethical philosophy may soon assist investors not only with *what* to do, but *why* to do it. Recommendation systems may evolve to simulate not just market outcomes, but the societal implications of those outcomes. The question will no longer be, "What's the expected return?" but, "What's the consequence profile of this decision?"

This is not science fiction. It is the logical extension of reframing money as data and investing as meaning-making. We are entering an age where *the data is no longer outside us*—it *includes* us. Our values, our stories, our ethical frameworks—all are inputs. And the most powerful portfolios will not only be optimised for profit, but for coherence with the world the investor wants to help build.

Because ultimately, the value of money lies not in what it can buy, but in *what it says.*

## Entropy, Uncertainty, and the Market

*How Physics and Chaos Theory Illuminate—and Complicate—AI's Approach to Financial Systems*

There's a quiet arrogance embedded in most financial models: a presumption that markets can be tamed into order. This confidence is not new—it is inherited from a lineage of thinkers who, borrowing from Newtonian mechanics, believed that with enough data and mathematical ingenuity, the market could be rendered predictable, like a clock whose gears merely required mapping. Yet beneath the veneer of volatility indexes, pricing models, and VaR tables lies a deeper truth—one that aligns less with mechanics and more with thermodynamics. Markets, like weather systems or biological ecosystems, are fundamentally entropic. They resist compression. They generate disorder even as we attempt to impose logic. And in this truth lies the tension between financial modelling and financial reality.

Artificial intelligence now stands at the forefront of this struggle. Where traditional risk models stumble in the face of emergent phenomena, AI promises adaptability. Machine learning algorithms, in particular, are lauded for their ability to 'learn' from data rather than rely on hard-coded rules. But can an algorithm truly make sense of systems that are defined by uncertainty? More provocatively: can AI ever move beyond prediction to understanding?

This chapter examines how the lens of physics—especially concepts like entropy, non-linearity, and chaos—provides a more honest frame for understanding both markets and the limits of the machines we design to navigate them.

### From Equilibrium to Chaos: The Market as a Complex System

Conventional economic theory has long rested on equilibrium thinking: the idea that markets, like pendulums, may swing but eventually return to balance. Such assumptions gave rise to tools like the Efficient Market Hypothesis (EMH), the Capital Asset Pricing Model (CAPM), and the Gaussian distribution of returns—all elegant, all flawed. In reality, markets exhibit *complex adaptive behaviour*. Price movements are shaped not merely by fundamentals, but by reflexivity, feedback loops, and irrational sentiment. Much like weather, they can evolve from stable to storm-like conditions without obvious triggers.

This is where physics—particularly thermodynamics—enters the conversation. Entropy, defined in physics as a measure of disorder or the number of possible microstates in a system, has a financial analogue. Every new trade, geopolitical headline, earnings call, or interest rate decision adds information (and therefore potential disorder) to the system. Markets don't evolve toward stasis; they evolve toward increasing complexity.

The challenge, then, is epistemological: how do you model what is, by nature, partially unknowable?

### AI and the Allure of Order

AI's appeal in this landscape is intuitive. Traditional risk models, calibrated to historical data, falter when the future deviates from the past. AI, by contrast, claims to detect latent patterns invisible to the human eye. Deep learning systems can process vast streams of structured and unstructured data—from satellite images to voice tone in earnings calls—and output probabilistic forecasts. Reinforcement learning models, trained on simulations, can dynamically rebalance portfolios in response to new inputs.

But here's the rub: even the most sophisticated AI models operate within constraints. They require *training data*, and that data is drawn from a reality that is already contingent, path-dependent, and noisy. AI does not eliminate uncertainty; it reshapes how we confront it. At best, AI provides a map of probabilities, not certainties—a probabilistic topography of a financial landscape that can, and often does, rearrange itself mid-navigation.

This distinction is crucial. While AI may outperform human traders in short-term arbitrage or high-frequency contexts, it remains vulnerable to *model fragility*—the risk that its assumptions break under rare or extreme conditions. When the system goes off-script, AI doesn't improvise. It recalculates. That may sound rigorous, but it is not the same as reasoning.

### Entropy as an Investment Variable

Entropy, when viewed through the lens of information theory, offers a powerful insight into investing: it is not just a backdrop to be managed, but a variable to be incorporated. The economist George Gilder once remarked that wealth is knowledge, and growth is learning. By this logic, markets thrive not because they are efficient, but because they are messy—because they absorb and transmit information, even imperfectly.

Investors, then, are not mere consumers of data but participants in an unfolding narrative. Every decision—whether to buy, hold, or sell—injects new information into the system, thereby increasing its entropy. Paradoxically, more data does not always lead to more clarity. In fact, the more we know, the more unstable our models can become, a phenomenon known in the social sciences as *epistemic overconfidence*.

This is where human intuition and machine computation must diverge. AI is brilliant at recognising statistical regularities. Humans, however, are better at *reframing the question.* When the facts no longer fit the model, the human investor can step back, reconsider, recontextualise. The algorithm cannot.

### Chaos Theory and the Myth of Repeatability

One of the most misunderstood yet relevant concepts from physics is *sensitive dependence on initial conditions*, popularly known as the Butterfly Effect. Coined in chaos theory, it suggests that small differences in starting inputs can yield vastly different outcomes. This principle holds especially true in markets, where fractional shifts in sentiment or policy can cascade into global dislocations.

Machine learning, by design, attempts to uncover repeatable patterns. But the very premise of chaos theory challenges that pursuit. What if the future is not a variation of the past, but something qualitatively new? What if the market's behaviour is contingent not just on economics, but on collective psychology, political asymmetry, or ecological shocks?

AI, trained on yesterday, may be blind to tomorrow's narrative shift. The 2008 financial crisis and the COVID-19 pandemic are often cited as *black swans*—highly improbable events with massive consequences. But what they also illustrate is the brittleness of models that presume stability. AI, no matter how nimble, is still fundamentally backward-looking in its training. It optimises for the expected. But history is made by the unexpected.

### Implications for Investors

So what are we to do in light of this complexity? First, we must abandon the illusion that risk can be fully modelled. The desire to reduce the market to an equation is not just unrealistic—it is dangerous. Second, we must reframe AI not as a sovereign strategist, but as an adaptive tool. It excels in certain terrains—namely, those with high data volume, clear feedback, and repeatable patterns. It falters in low-frequency, high-impact domains—areas that demand interpretation, imagination, and judgement.

Finally, we must acknowledge the irreplaceable role of human meta-cognition. The ability to *question the model itself*—to recognise when our tools are no longer fit for purpose—is arguably the highest form of intelligence in uncertain systems. AI can adjust parameters; humans can redefine paradigms.

In embracing AI, let us not outsource our thinking, but extend it. Entropy will always be with us. The goal is not to eliminate uncertainty, but to become wiser about where it lives—and where it hides.

## Narratives vs. Numbers

*Reckoning with the Two Languages of Modern Investing*

If modern investing has a central paradox, it is this: the better we become at quantifying the world, the more power stories seem to hold. Despite advances in machine learning, behavioural analytics, and the proliferation of data, the market remains deeply human—a stage where numbers inform, but narratives decide. Investors are told to trust the data, to be rational, to model their portfolios like engineers calibrate machinery. And yet markets still surge on sentiment, pivot on perception, and move not always in response to new information, but to new interpretations of old information. This tension—between empiricism and storytelling—lies at the heart of how we think about money, risk, and value.

In the age of AI, the stakes of this tension have sharpened. Algorithms can now ingest terabytes of structured and unstructured data, from economic indicators to Twitter sentiment. They can model scenarios, back-test strategies, and respond to signals at speeds no human can match. But they cannot believe. They do not construct meaning. They don't create context. Humans, by contrast, are narrative creatures. We invest not only in returns but in futures we imagine. We buy not only equity, but identity. Reconciling these two forces—the rigour of data and the resonance of story—is not just a challenge for investors; it is the challenge of investing in the twenty-first century.

## The Allure of the Story

Human cognition evolved to understand the world through cause and effect. We are wired to detect patterns and impose coherence. When faced with complexity, we reach for stories: simplified, often moralised accounts that allow us to make sense of uncertainty. In finance, this explains why narratives shape behaviour even when data contradicts them. It's why the "Tesla story" or the "China growth miracle" can drive asset prices more powerfully than quarterly earnings or discounted cash flow models.

Consider the 2020s boom in ESG investing. For many institutions, environmental and social metrics defy clean quantification—yet the *story* of sustainable investing resonates. Investors allocate capital not just to optimise risk-adjusted returns, but to participate in a collective identity shift. Similarly, crypto assets, which lack traditional valuation anchors, have thrived on powerful narratives of decentralisation, technological liberation, and monetary rebellion. These stories activate emotional circuitry, frame risk in moral rather than statistical terms, and ultimately shape investor demand.

Stories can also serve as psychological defence mechanisms. Losses are rationalised as temporary setbacks in a long-term thesis. Market exuberance is justified through transformational visions. This narrative resilience can be productive—it supports conviction in the face of volatility—but it can also be dangerous. It leads to confirmation bias, herding behaviour, and the tendency to overfit reality to an internally consistent, but externally flawed, worldview.

### The Case for Numbers

Against this narrative bias stands the disciplined counterweight of data. Numbers anchor decisions in evidence. They impose constraints on speculation. In theory, quantitative investing offers a way to strip emotion out of markets and approach asset allocation with clinical objectivity.

AI-driven platforms now take this logic further. Using neural networks, natural language processing, and reinforcement learning, they attempt to find statistical relationships that elude human intuition. These systems don't "believe" in a story—they merely optimise for outcomes based on input variables. Their edge lies not in interpretation, but in iteration. A human might update a thesis quarterly; an algorithm can do so millisecond by millisecond. In domains with high information velocity and repeatable patterns—like options pricing or short-term arbitrage—machines outperform by orders of magnitude.

However, this strength is also a limitation. AI is inherently reactive. It extrapolates from what is, not from what could be. It cannot "see around corners" unless the data teaches it to do so. It does not question its own assumptions unless explicitly instructed. And most critically, it cannot generate original hypotheses about why a pattern matters—or when a statistically significant trend is actually *meaningless*.

Moreover, reliance on numbers creates its own form of blindness. Quant models often obscure the assumptions baked into their design. Backtests can produce false confidence. Correlations can masquerade as causations. And in periods of market discontinuity—black swan events, regime changes, or paradigm shifts—quantitative systems trained on yesterday's data may misfire entirely.

### A False Binary

Framing this as a contest—numbers versus narratives—misses the point. The real sophistication lies in integration. The best investors are not those who reject story for data, or data for story, but those who can *navigate the space between.* They ask: what is the prevailing narrative, and what data supports or undermines it? Where is the disconnect between sentiment and substance? What stories are priced in, and which are poised to surprise?

This synthesis is not purely philosophical; it has practical implications. Consider venture capital. Early-stage investing is largely narrative-driven—there are no profits, limited metrics, and vast uncertainty. But within that fog, data still plays a role: unit economics, market sizing, cohort analysis. The narrative may excite, but the numbers must justify entry and support scaling decisions. Conversely, in highly liquid markets, where quantitative factors dominate, it is often narrative shifts—central bank rhetoric, political crises, technological breakthroughs—that produce inflection points in asset prices.

### Constructing Narrative Literacy

If investors are to operate effectively in this dual-language environment, they must cultivate *narrative literacy.* This means understanding not only how stories function, but how they evolve. Narratives follow arcs: rise, crescendo, saturation, and collapse. They are shaped by metaphors, analogies, and archetypes. They are vulnerable to mutation and co-option. And critically, they are amplified or dampened by media, social networks, and influencer economies.

Narrative literacy also requires *historical perspective.* Financial storytelling is not new. From Dutch tulips to railroad stocks, dot-coms to housing bubbles, markets have long oscillated between rational optimism and speculative delusion. Recognising these patterns doesn't prevent irrationality, but it can temper its impact.

Investors who can place today's hype in the context of yesterday's cycles are less likely to mistake noise for signal.

And finally, narrative literacy demands *ethical awareness*. Stories are not neutral. They carry values, power dynamics, and political consequences. When a narrative promotes short-term profit at the expense of long-term sustainability—or erases externalities for the sake of quarterly earnings—it is not only misleading but potentially destructive. Data can lie, but stories can justify the lie. The investor's responsibility is not only to interpret both, but to interrogate their implications.

### The Path Forward

To invest wisely today is to hold a dialectic between precision and perception. It is to engage with data as a necessary—but not sufficient—guide. It is to embrace stories as context—but not gospel. The AI revolution makes this balance even more urgent. As machines get better at modelling the world, humans must get better at *modelling meaning.*

The tools may change. The pace will accelerate. But the core challenge remains the same: to distinguish the plausible from the probable, the compelling from the true. Investors who master both languages—numbers and narrative—will not merely survive in the noise. They will decode it.

## Investing in Meaning, Not Just Return

*Why the Future of Capital Requires More Than Capital Gains*

The traditional investor's question—*what will this return?*—is giving way to a more complex inquiry: *what will this return mean?* For decades, modern portfolio theory reduced investing to a clean equation: maximise returns, minimise risk. Wealth was an outcome, measured in numbers. The future, if considered at all, was discounted to present value. But as global challenges intensify—climate instability, rising inequality, political polarisation—investors are confronting a truth that economists long kept outside the model: capital does not exist in a vacuum. It shapes, and is shaped by, the world around it. What you fund, you feed. Where you invest, you influence. And increasingly, the returns people seek are not just financial—they are moral, social, ecological, and cultural.

This shift is not cosmetic. It's a structural rethinking of what investing *is*. It moves the conversation from extraction to contribution. From accumulation to alignment. From asking *how much?* to asking *what for?* And while this movement has gained traction under labels like ESG, impact investing, and stakeholder capitalism, these terms are often misunderstood, misapplied, or prematurely dismissed. The deeper question they gesture toward remains largely unresolved: *what does it mean to make money meaningfully?*

### The False Binary of Profit and Purpose

One of the most persistent myths in finance is the trade-off narrative—that doing good must come at the expense of doing well. The phrase "fiduciary duty" has too often been wielded as a shield for short-termism, as if profit and principle were mutually exclusive. In reality, this binary is intellectually outdated and empirically weak. Study after study—from MSCI, Morningstar, Harvard Business School, and beyond—has found that firms with high sustainability scores often outperform over the long term. Why? Because they manage risk better, attract and retain better talent, and are more attuned to shifting regulatory and consumer landscapes.

Consider renewable energy. A decade ago, solar was pitched as a feel-good investment with modest returns. Today, it's a dominant theme in global infrastructure portfolios. Or look at diversity. Companies with diverse leadership teams aren't just more equitable—they tend to be more innovative, more resilient, and more reflective of their customer base. Purpose, when intelligently embedded, is not a concession. It's a *competitive advantage.*

## The Rise of the Conscious Capital Allocator

The new generation of investors—millennials, Gen Z, mission-driven institutions—are not content to make money and donate later. They want alignment now. They expect transparency, accountability, and coherence between the values they live by and the assets they hold. This has profound implications for the financial services industry, which must evolve from product provider to values translator.

Tools are emerging to support this shift. AI-based portfolio design can now score companies not only on their balance sheets but on their carbon footprints, governance practices, or social impact. Natural language processing is used to analyse proxy statements and detect greenwashing. Platforms like Ethic and OpenInvest allow users to customise portfolios around causes, not just sectors—be it racial justice, gender equity, or refugee support. The result is a personalisation of capital that mirrors the rise of personalisation in every other domain, from medicine to media.

But technology is only part of the story. What matters more is intention. The best algorithms are still bounded by the priorities we encode into them. Purpose-led investing is not about outsourcing ethics to data science. It's about reclaiming agency in a system that too often rewards detachment.

## Rethinking Risk in an Interconnected World

Traditional finance models treat risk as volatility—as the standard deviation of returns. But this narrow view misses systemic and existential risks: climate collapse, biodiversity loss, supply chain fragility, political instability. These are not exogenous "black swans"; they are endogenous consequences of how capital has been allocated. To invest in meaning is to redefine risk as *disconnection from reality*—economic, ecological, and human.

The COVID-19 pandemic made this starkly clear. Portfolios that appeared diversified on paper were exposed as fragile in practice. What they lacked was not asset-class dispersion, but *resilience.* Investors who had integrated ESG factors—particularly in areas like labour practices, employee safety, and supply chain ethics—weathered the storm better. This was not charity. It was prudence.

The lesson is enduring: in a tightly coupled world, externalities become internalities faster than models predict. Climate risk is financial risk. Social unrest is market risk. Ethical myopia is portfolio risk. To manage these risks requires more than Monte Carlo simulations. It demands moral imagination.

### Toward an Integrated Investment Philosophy

The move toward meaning is not a repudiation of returns. It is a *redefinition* of what constitutes a worthwhile return. This demands a shift from transactional thinking to relational thinking. From linear cause-effect models to complex systems thinking. From quarterly earnings to generational stewardship.

To lead in this new landscape, investors must develop *multidimensional fluency*—the ability to weigh not just financial upside, but cultural signal, ecological consequence, and reputational arc. They must learn to ask:

What kind of future does this investment accelerate?

Who benefits, and who bears the cost?

Is this enterprise extractive, neutral, or regenerative?

If this strategy succeeds, will the world be better for it?

These questions are not rhetorical. They are diagnostic. They sharpen decision-making. They uncover hidden risk. And they create the possibility of a portfolio that is not only profitable, but meaningful.

### The Ethical Edge

As algorithms automate more of the tactical layer—optimisation, rebalancing, tax loss harvesting—the strategic layer becomes increasingly human. Ethics, long-term vision, and contextual judgment cannot be hardcoded. They must be cultivated. In this light, ethics is not a constraint on investing. It is a form of insight. It is the ability to see consequences that others miss and to act in ways that endure.

This is where human intelligence can—and must—outperform artificial intelligence. The investor of the future is not simply a quantitative analyst or a behavioural economist. They are a *philosopher with a spreadsheet.* A systems thinker with skin in the game. An architect of capital with the humility to ask not just *what will this earn?* but *what will this enable?*

Ultimately, the pursuit of meaningful investing is not about perfect purity. It is about conscious compromise. It is about making money *in a way that makes sense*—to the world, to society, and to oneself. This is not a trend. It is a realignment. The most influential capital in the coming decades will be the kind that builds coherence between values and value, between data and dignity.

If finance is the language of the future, let's ensure it speaks clearly, honestly, and humanely. Let us invest not only in assets, but in outcomes. Not only in instruments, but in impact. And let us remember that behind every allocation is a belief about the kind of world we think is worth building.

# Chapter 6
# Emotional Algorithms and Psychological Traps

When Investing Becomes a Battle Between the Brain and the Code

If an algorithm could feel, it wouldn't behave anything like us. It wouldn't twitch at a sudden dip in the markets, wouldn't cling to the latest investment fad or mistake the familiar for the safe. Nor would it overestimate its forecasting prowess after a stroke of blind luck. FOMO, pride, panic—these are ghosts that don't haunt machines. That absence of emotional clutter offers a certain cold efficiency: consistency without second-guessing, pattern recognition stripped of bias. But that's only half the story. Human investors, for all their flaws, bring something else to the table—something messier, yes, but textured with depth. We don't invest solely with logic or odds. We invest with identity, with feeling, with the tangled narratives we whisper to ourselves.

Investing now plays out on a more psychological terrain than ever before. It's no longer just a matter of strategy, spreadsheets, or sophisticated models. It has become a struggle of the self: the human mind pitted against the unblinking precision of code; instinct grappling with machine discipline; story clashing with statistics. As technology increasingly assumes the role of the impassive, rational actor, our own emotional architecture becomes not just relevant, but pivotal. Not because we imagine we might outwit the machines, but because we must first stop outwitting ourselves.

This chapter turns inward—to examine a force as pervasive as any market trend, yet rarely scrutinised with the same rigour: the investor's own cognitive machinery. Our brains, fine-tuned for immediacy and survival, falter when faced with the long, uncertain arc of capital growth. Ironically, the very tools we now rely on to help us navigate this terrain—the apps, feeds, platforms—are calibrated to provoke. They aren't designed to encourage stillness or thoughtful re-evaluation. They are built to trigger. While the machine reacts to probabilities, the human responds to hope, fear, and the jolt of intuition half-formed.

And yet, there's a kind of advantage in knowing just how outmatched we can be—not to despair, but to intervene. Over the past two decades, behavioural finance and decision science have traced the contours of our mental misfires. Confirmation bias, loss aversion, the compulsion to act when doing nothing might be wiser—these are not minor quirks. They're systemic glitches in the way we're wired. But awareness makes space. Even a sliver of distance between stimulus and response can be invaluable. That pause—that moment where habit yields to reflection—may prove our greatest asset.

We begin, then, with first principles: how decisions are formed, why risk can feel far more threatening than it looks on a spreadsheet, and how ambiguity often befuddles even the most seasoned investor. Emotions aren't mere accessories to decision-making; they permeate it, often steering the wheel before we even notice. Add to this the rise of interfaces powered by AI, and the game shifts. Brokerage apps, once tools, now resemble casinos—slick, gamified, compulsively clickable. With a flick of the thumb, we can check our portfolio—and feel its rise or fall in the gut.

From this vantage, we explore the predictable traps we fall into, again and again. Overconfidence isn't merely bravado—it's a skewed reading of skill versus luck. It leads to excess trading, to premature exits, to misunderstood risk. Then there's the illusion of control—believing we're at the helm, even as algorithms do the heavy lifting behind the curtain. Perhaps most deceptively, there's emotional reasoning: the impulse to weave meaning into data not because it's warranted, but because it soothes or excites us. And ironically, the more data we absorb, the greater the temptation to interpret it through our own stories.

This leads us to a recurring tension: the very qualities that make us human—imagination, empathy, aversion to loss—also expose us to poor decisions. The goal, however, isn't to strip these things away. It's to sharpen them. The latter part of this chapter turns practical—not with gimmicks or clever mental shortcuts, but with deeper disciplines. Cognitive re-framing. Identifying emotional cues. Developing habits of reflection. Like any well-trained algorithm, we too can learn to recognise patterns—within ourselves.

Where the previous chapter positioned metacognition as a uniquely human gift, this one moves from theory to application. It's about the everyday challenge of regulating one's inner landscape while navigating systems designed to amplify every emotional ripple. We're not detached minds operating in a vacuum. We are status-conscious, loss-averse, wired for reaction—and immersed in environments that capitalise on precisely those traits.

But let's not mistake this as a condemnation of emotion. Emotions have their own intelligence. They reveal priorities, expose vulnerabilities, highlight what matters most. The trouble is not that we feel—but that we fail to interpret those feelings with clarity. Emotions, left unexamined, blur the signal. The task isn't to suppress them, but to listen, question, and decide with intent. That's not just about discipline. It requires mental lucidity.

This chapter doesn't argue that investing must be purged of emotion. It contends, rather, that emotion left unscrutinised is where risk truly lives. Like faulty code, beliefs can be debugged. In this age of automated execution and algorithmic foresight, the real edge lies elsewhere—not in faster calculations, but in a richer understanding of one's own cognitive terrain. The best investors aren't just adept with numbers. They've learned to draw a line between instinct and impulse—and to construct a process that honours that distinction.

Markets will always be complex, confounding, unpredictable. The machines will grow swifter, more persuasive. But one thing remains stubbornly, refreshingly human: the ability to observe oneself—to adapt not just to the market, but to one's own patterns. That's the advantage worth cultivating. Not through spreadsheets, but through the quiet, continuous act of self-awareness turned into strategy.

## Your Brain vs. the Bot

*How Emotional Circuitry Distorts Investment—and What Machines Do Differently*

There's a persistent misconception that access to data alone makes us better investors. It doesn't. If anything, our expanding informational landscape exposes a deeper truth: human irrationality is stubbornly immune to statistics. While we like to imagine ourselves as rational actors navigating markets with objectivity, neuroeconomics has repeatedly shown otherwise. Our investment decisions are filtered not through spreadsheets, but through the limbic system—wired for survival, not for compounding interest. And here lies the defining contrast between us and the machines we've built to out-think us.

AI systems don't get spooked by market volatility. They don't chase rallies or panic during sell-offs. They don't suffer from confirmation bias, loss aversion, or the dangerous euphoria of recency. They have no evolutionary baggage to contend with. In this sense, the great asymmetry in modern investing is not just informational—it's *emotional.* The edge that bots have over human investors lies less in speed and more in psychological immunity. That raises an uncomfortable question: If emotion is our liability, how do we compete?

To answer this, we must first understand how emotion—specifically fear, reward, and narrative construction—shapes our economic decisions.

### The Biology of Bias: When the Brain Becomes a Market Liability

At the heart of neuroeconomics lies a simple but profound insight: *the brain cannot distinguish between financial risk and physical danger.* When you see your portfolio drop 10%, your amygdala lights up as if you've just spotted a predator. Cortisol floods the bloodstream. Rational thought narrows. This cascade of biological responses—adaptive in the Pleistocene—can be catastrophic in a modern asset allocation context.

Take loss aversion, a concept rooted in prospect theory and confirmed through fMRI research. The brain's response to financial loss is stronger than its response to an equivalent gain. This creates a predictable pattern: investors hold onto losing stocks far longer than is rational, hoping to "get even," while prematurely selling winners to lock in gains. The machine, on the other hand, obeys no such heuristics. It exits based on signal degradation, not emotional discomfort.

Overconfidence is another deep-seated cognitive flaw. Studies consistently show that individual investors overrate their abilities, under-diversify their holdings, and trade too frequently. Algorithms, in contrast, operate with calibrated humility. They update beliefs probabilistically, adjust continuously, and never confuse intuition with insight. This isn't merely a technical difference—it's a philosophical one. AI doesn't need to "believe" in a position. It just needs the data to justify it.

**Dopamine Loops and Digital Platforms: The Engineered Investor Experience**

It's not just biology that traps us. Increasingly, it's also interface. Trading apps, portfolio dashboards, and real-time alerts are designed to hijack our attention. Robinhood's now-infamous use of gamification—confetti after trades, dopamine-triggering visual feedback, and colour-coded volatility cues—doesn't just make investing accessible; it makes it addictive. These are not neutral tools. They're behavioural manipulation engines disguised as innovation.

AI, by contrast, does not care whether the interface is delightful or dull. It doesn't check prices compulsively. It doesn't need to "feel in control." The dispassionate execution of an algorithm stands in stark contrast to the feedback loops that keep human investors perpetually reactive.

What emerges, then, is an uncomfortable reality: the platforms we use often amplify the very biases we should be trying to suppress. In this sense, behavioural design becomes a risk factor—not unlike leverage or exposure—except it sits inside our phones, not our portfolios.

## Machines That Learn, Humans That Rationalise

Artificial intelligence isn't magic. Its core strength is *pattern recognition.* Trained on millions of historical datapoints, machine learning models identify subtle relationships invisible to the human eye. But what makes these systems formidable isn't just their scale—it's their lack of ego. An AI doesn't try to defend its prior assumptions. It simply adjusts. If yesterday's strategy no longer works, the model evolves. Humans, by contrast, rationalise poor decisions to protect a coherent self-narrative.

This cognitive dissonance explains why intelligent investors can persist in flawed strategies for years. They don't lack IQ—they lack epistemic humility. They conflate conviction with accuracy. Algorithms are free from this burden. They're not committed to being right. They're committed to updating.

But here's the twist: while AI models can self-correct, they're only as good as the frameworks we give them. They need human architects to define objective functions, constrain parameters, and evaluate fairness. A flawed data pipeline or improperly tuned model can lead to systemic errors that go unchallenged—simply because the machine is executing precisely as instructed.

## The Human Advantage: Awareness, Adaptation, and Meta-Cognition

This brings us to a critical pivot point. Emotionality is a weakness—but not an absolute one. What separates thoughtful investors from impulsive ones isn't the absence of emotion, but *the awareness of its influence.* Neuroeconomics does not advocate for Spock-like detachment. It calls for *meta-cognition*: the ability to think about how we think, to step back from the first-order impulse and engage the reflective mind.

This is where humans still retain an edge. We can *question our frameworks*, not just our forecasts. We can ask whether a strategy aligns with our values, whether a risk is worth bearing, or whether a signal has ethical implications beyond its Sharpe ratio. The machine can optimise returns—but it cannot contemplate meaning.

AI can execute a strategy with perfect precision. It cannot tell you whether that strategy *should* be executed.

In this sense, the most powerful human investors of the future won't be those who try to outcompute the machines. It will be those who *design better questions*, who interpret algorithmic output with psychological literacy, and who balance cold execution with ethical intentionality.

## Toward Hybrid Mastery: Where Behavioural Science Meets Algorithmic Precision

The path forward is not to abandon the machine, nor to outsource judgment entirely. It is to *build a cognitive alliance.* Imagine an investment workflow where the algorithm runs a thousand simulations—but you decide which ones matter. Where your bias-aware dashboard flags when you're trading emotionally. Where your decision journal logs not just what you did, but why—and whether your rationale evolved.

These tools already exist in primitive form. Behavioural nudges embedded in trading platforms. AI-driven alerts that detect impulsive trading patterns. Journaling apps that tag cognitive fallacies. But their real power lies not in technology, but in *philosophy*: the belief that investing should be not just efficient, but reflective.

### Final Insight: The Future Is Not Either/Or

As artificial intelligence becomes embedded in every layer of finance—from strategy design to execution and even compliance—the human investor faces a crossroads. Compete emotionally and you will lose. But *collaborate intelligently* and you gain a powerful new edge: the ability to bring depth, ethics, and meaning to a system optimised for speed and scale.

This is not the death of the human investor. It is their redefinition. The bot will never fear, never hope, never reflect. But it also will never *care*. And that makes all the difference.

## Fear, Greed, and Dopamine Loops: How Platforms Hack Investor Behaviour—and How to Reclaim Control

There's a reason your thumb hovers compulsively over your trading app. A reason the flashing green of a rising stock induces a subtle rush, while a red plunge triggers a sinking dread in your gut. These reactions are not incidental—they are engineered. In today's investment landscape, platforms are no longer just neutral tools for executing trades. They are behavioural laboratories that understand your psychology often better than you do. At the heart of this manipulation lies a powerful biological currency: dopamine.

What was once a domain dominated by suits, spreadsheets, and stoicism has, in recent years, adopted the skin of a digital casino. Trading apps now blend gamification, algorithmic nudging, and continuous stimulation to keep investors engaged, reactive, and—crucially—addicted. Understanding how these systems exploit our brain's reward circuitry isn't merely an academic exercise; it is a vital step in regaining control of our financial agency in an age of algorithmic persuasion.

### The Biochemistry of Market Behaviour

To begin with, we must appreciate that human beings are not rational calculators. The notion of Homo economicus—logical, self-maximising, unemotional—has long been debunked by behavioural economics and cognitive neuroscience. Instead, we are creatures of habit, emotion, and cognitive shortcuts. Nowhere is this more evident than in the act of trading.

At the neurobiological level, investing activates the same reward system that governs food, sex, and social affirmation. Dopamine, a neurotransmitter associated with anticipation and pleasure, spikes not when a reward is received, but when it is expected. It's the thrill of *maybe*. This anticipatory loop is what makes slot machines addictive—and it's precisely what's being replicated in modern investment platforms.

Each swipe, each flickering price chart, each push notification is a variable reward trigger. Like Skinner's pigeons pressing levers in unpredictable reward schedules, investors are trained to engage in behaviour patterns that prioritise short-term gratification over long-term strategy.

### Fear and Greed: The Twin Tyrants of the Market

The market is often described as a pendulum swinging between two primal forces: fear and greed. But this metaphor, while widely used, obscures a deeper reality. Fear and greed are not just market sentiments; they are ancient survival mechanisms encoded in the brain.

Greed, or reward-seeking behaviour, is driven largely by dopaminergic activity in the nucleus accumbens. It makes investors chase highs—both psychological and financial. It fuels overconfidence, encourages speculative bubbles, and creates momentum frenzies where fundamentals are ignored.

Fear, on the other hand, is a defensive response. It resides in the amygdala and is closely tied to loss aversion—a phenomenon where the pain of losing is roughly twice as powerful as the pleasure of gaining. Losses loom larger, and thus provoke more irrational action.

Investors panic-sell at the bottom and buy exuberantly at the top, not because they are foolish, but because their neurobiology is wired that way.

Platforms, whether intentionally or incidentally, often stoke these emotions. Volatility alerts, dramatic headlines, and end-of-day performance summaries can catalyse fear responses. Conversely, celebratory graphics, "You're up today!" badges, and social comparison features amplify greed.

## The Platform as Behavioural Engineer

It is not a stretch to say that modern trading platforms act as digital choice architects. They shape how information is presented, which options are emphasised, and how frequently users are nudged to engage. This behavioural design is not merely aesthetic; it is strategic.

Consider *Robinhood*, one of the most scrutinised trading platforms in recent years. With its use of confetti animations, colourful interfaces, and commission-free trading, it lowered not just the financial cost of trading—but the psychological friction. What might have once felt like a weighty decision now felt like a mobile game. Research shows that such gamified environments increase frequency of trades, often at the expense of portfolio performance.

Moreover, many platforms harvest behavioural data to refine their nudges. If you tend to buy after market rallies, or sell after dips, algorithms will learn your patterns and may "personalise" the way you're alerted or prompted. The result is a feedback loop not of rational reflection, but of reactive engagement.

## The Cost of Continuous Stimulation

Ironically, the more we are stimulated by the market, the less intelligent our investing becomes. High-frequency engagement leads to emotional decision-making, myopic loss aversion, and short-term bias. The constant dopamine-seeking cycle crowds out the slower, more deliberate modes of thinking that characterise wise financial judgment.

Psychologist Daniel Kahneman's "System 1" and "System 2" model is particularly apt here. System 1 is fast, instinctive, and emotional—perfect for reacting to a falling stock price or a breaking news alert. System 2 is slower, analytical, and effortful—better suited for assessing a company's fundamentals or evaluating long-term strategy. Trading platforms are designed to keep you in System 1 mode as often as possible.

This shift is not without consequence. Studies show that overtrading is a major drag on returns. A 2011 analysis published in *The Journal of Finance* found that retail investors who traded more frequently earned significantly lower returns than those who traded less often, a phenomenon attributed to behavioural biases and transaction costs—both exacerbated by dopamine loops.

**Reclaiming Control: From Pavlovian to Principled**

If the system is rigged to exploit our emotional circuitry, the solution is not to abandon the market, but to reassert agency within it. This begins with *meta-cognition*—the ability to observe and question one's own mental processes. Recognising when you are in a reactive state is the first defence against manipulation.

One effective strategy is to implement *deliberate friction.* This could mean removing trading apps from your phone, instituting a 24-hour cooling-off period before making trades, or maintaining a written investment thesis that must be consulted before each decision. These small design choices act as psychological brakes, giving System 2 a fighting chance to intervene.

Another essential tool is *journaling.* Keeping a record of not only what you did, but *why* you did it, helps reveal patterns of impulsivity and emotional reactivity. Over time, this builds a form of behavioural accountability that data analytics alone cannot provide.

Finally, consider cultivating a *values-based investing framework*. When your portfolio is anchored to long-term goals and ethical convictions—rather than momentary signals—it becomes more resilient to emotional turbulence. Purpose, it turns out, is an excellent antidote to panic.

### The Investor as Designer, Not Just Participant

The future of investing will not be won by those who can out-calculate the machines. It will be won by those who can out-think them—not in computational power, but in *cognitive clarity*. In a world of engineered temptation, the new investing edge is not faster execution, but deeper reflection.

To regain control is to redesign not only your tools, but your mind. To understand that trading platforms are not neutral, and neither is your psychology. To realise that every flicker on a screen is a potential trigger—and every decision an opportunity to practise discipline.

Fear and greed may be part of human nature, but they need not be our masters. With awareness, structure, and intention, the investor can reclaim their sovereignty—not by rejecting emotion, but by understanding its architecture and choosing wisely how to act upon it.

## The Illusion of Control: Why Overconfidence Persists in the Age of Predictive Precision

There is perhaps no greater paradox in modern investing than this: the more data we have, the more confident we become—and the less accurate our decisions often are. This is not a failure of technology. It is a failure of cognition. In a world awash with predictive analytics, machine-generated insights, and real-time dashboards, many investors operate under a potent and persistent delusion: that more information equals more control. It does not.

The illusion of control is not simply a behavioural quirk—it is a cognitive distortion with profound implications for financial decision-making. Even in the most sophisticated, data-rich environments, investors systematically overestimate their ability to forecast outcomes, manage risk, and influence results. The tragedy is not just that we are wrong, but that we are wrong with conviction.

Understanding this phenomenon is more than a psychological exercise. It is an urgent intellectual task for anyone who seeks to invest wisely in the age of algorithmic assistance.

## The Origins of the Illusion

Coined by psychologist Ellen Langer in the 1970s, the "illusion of control" refers to the tendency for people to overestimate their influence over events that are actually governed by chance. Langer's famous experiments showed that individuals believed they had a better chance of winning a lottery when they selected their own numbers, even when the process was objectively random.

What seems trivial in a game becomes deeply consequential in the market. Investors often mistake correlation for causation, experience for expertise, and agency for accuracy. This cognitive bias persists because it offers a sense of comfort—an antidote to uncertainty. In volatile or ambiguous environments, the brain seeks patterns, even where none exist, and clings to control as a defence against chaos.

## Overconfidence in a Quantified World

It is tempting to assume that the rise of AI, machine learning, and big data would correct these biases by offering a more objective lens on the world. But the opposite often occurs. As the complexity of financial systems increases, so too does the human tendency to seek simplified narratives of control. Access to more granular information gives the *illusion* of greater mastery, even as systems grow more opaque and unpredictable.

Consider the modern investor armed with a portfolio dashboard that updates in real-time, with volatility models, beta coefficients, sentiment indicators, and macroeconomic overlays. One might assume such sophistication leads to better decisions. And yet, empirical studies consistently show that excessive data often leads to *overtrading*, *miscalibrated forecasts*, and *amplified risk exposure*—all markers of overconfidence.

A 2006 study published in *The Journal of Finance* found that professional fund managers, despite their expertise and access to superior information, exhibited no better forecasting accuracy than randomised controls over multi-year periods. Yet they expressed significantly higher confidence in their predictions. The knowledge was abundant, but the humility was not.

### Data Does Not Equal Discernment

This cognitive trap is especially pronounced in the age of interactive platforms. The more tools we have at our fingertips, the more we feel we are "doing something"—adjusting allocations, tweaking strategies, hedging positions. This *activity bias* is fuelled by an illusion: that constant motion signals intelligent design.

But most variables in financial markets remain outside individual control—interest rates, geopolitical risk, macroeconomic cycles, and market sentiment are shaped by complex, often chaotic systems. Even with perfect information, outcomes remain probabilistic.

More disturbingly, access to AI-generated forecasts can compound the problem. Machine learning systems often identify non-linear, non-intuitive patterns that defy traditional economic logic. When these predictions align with our views, we feel validated. When they don't, we second-guess the machine, not ourselves.

This creates what behavioural economists call *algorithm aversion*: the tendency to override or abandon models—even superior ones—when they make mistakes that humans would also make. This bias reinforces the illusion of control by asserting the primacy of human intuition over statistical inference, even when the latter is demonstrably more accurate.

### The Persistence of Overconfidence

Overconfidence is not evenly distributed; it varies by domain, demographic, and experience level. Interestingly, research shows that those with *intermediate* levels of expertise tend to be most overconfident—a phenomenon known as the "Dunning-Kruger curve." Novices know they don't know; experts know the limits of their knowledge. It's those in between who are most likely to conflate familiarity with skill.

In investing, this means that a retail investor who has read a few whitepapers and experienced a few wins may be more dangerously overconfident than a seasoned quant who has seen models fail repeatedly. The illusion of control thrives not just on ignorance, but on partial knowledge, untempered by reflection.

This explains the prevalence of market misjudgements during speculative bubbles. In the lead-up to crashes—be it the dot-com era, the housing crisis, or the crypto surges—investors felt emboldened by recent gains, reinforced by data that appeared to validate their theses. But the models were only accurate until they weren't. Risk was hidden in plain sight, mispriced by belief.

### Why Risk Feels Safer Than It Is

Human beings are poor at intuitively grasping compound risk. This is especially true in environments that offer *feedback*, but not *correction*. If an investor takes a leveraged position that happens to perform well, the result reinforces the sense of control, even if the outcome was luck rather than skill. This is what Nassim Nicholas Taleb has called "noise-labelled-as-signal" in probabilistic systems.

Moreover, the emotional rewards of feeling in control are significant. Control is psychologically linked to agency, autonomy, and efficacy—traits that form the core of identity for many high-functioning professionals. To suggest that markets are uncontrollable, or that one's judgment is fallible, feels like a threat to the self.

This is why even after repeated losses or failed predictions, investors will often attribute poor outcomes to *external shocks* rather than internal misjudgment. The illusion of control is preserved by narrative—stories we tell ourselves to maintain coherence and confidence.

### Towards Intellectual Humility

The antidote to the illusion of control is not paralysis or passivity—it is *intellectual humility*. This does not mean abandoning models or surrendering judgment. Rather, it means acknowledging the limits of knowledge, and the stochastic nature of complex systems.

Practical strategies include:

**Pre-mortem analysis**: Before committing to a position, investors can imagine the trade has failed and work backwards to identify possible causes. This combats narrative fallacy and introduces risk-awareness.

**Bayesian thinking**: Updating beliefs incrementally based on new evidence—rather than clinging to fixed theses—improves calibration.

**Diversification of mental models**: Drawing from disciplines outside finance—psychology, ecology, statistics—reduces over-reliance on a single paradigm of control.

**Reflective journaling**: Tracking not just decisions, but reasoning, helps illuminate patterns of overconfidence over time.

Above all, investors must learn to separate *skill* from *structure*. Sometimes good decisions yield bad outcomes. Sometimes bad decisions are rewarded. In markets, as in life, noise and randomness are part of the terrain. Control is never absolute—it is partial, probabilistic, and always subject to revision.

### Reframing the Role of the Investor

To be an investor today is not merely to interpret data or build portfolios. It is to navigate an epistemic landscape filled with uncertainty, incentives, and illusion. The role of the modern investor is less that of a puppeteer pulling strings, and more that of a cartographer mapping a moving terrain—adaptable, empirical, and aware of the fog.

The illusion of control is seductive because it promises clarity. But true wisdom in investing lies in resisting that promise. In recognising that what matters most is not how much you know, but how well you adapt to what you *cannot* know.

In this light, humility is not weakness. It is a strategic advantage.

## Reprogramming the Inner Investor

*How to transition from reactive instincts to reflective intelligence in the age of machine-accelerated markets*

In today's markets, every twitch of the thumb—every trade, scroll, or swipe—can feel like action. We've confused *motion* for *mastery*, and noise for nuance. Investors are no longer just evaluating portfolios; they are managing themselves. Against a backdrop of real-time data, emotionally engineered platforms, and algorithmic competitors with no pulse and no pause, *self-regulation has become the new alpha*. But while machines trade on logic and latency, humans are built to flinch. This chapter confronts that vulnerability—and shows how to rewire it into strength.

The investor of the future will not merely be literate in finance or fluent in technology. They will need to be psychologically self-aware: capable of interrupting automatic impulses, reframing emotional distortions, and making decisions that are internally coherent as well as externally optimised. This shift—from reactive to reflective—is neither simple nor cosmetic. It demands a deeper reprogramming of the internal investor: a transformation that begins not with a screen, but with a mirror.

### Why Your Psychology is Now a Strategic Variable

In classical finance theory, the human investor was presumed rational. Information was assumed to be symmetrical, behaviour logical, and outcomes efficient. Reality has never complied. Decades of behavioural finance and neuroeconomics research have shown that decision-making is shaped by cognitive distortions, social mimicry, and affective volatility. And in today's environment, where algorithms surf volatility faster than humans can react, those distortions are magnified, not corrected.

Markets have become mirrors, not calculators—they reflect the behavioural biases of their participants as much as they price assets. When millions of investors respond simultaneously to digital signals—price movements, headlines, push notifications—they don't just react to the market; they amplify it. In this environment, *psychological discipline is not an advantage—it's a necessity.*

This is where reprogramming begins: not by eliminating emotion, but by learning to observe, interrupt, and ultimately redesign its influence.

### The Brain's Architecture Isn't Built for Investing—But It Can Be Trained

The prefrontal cortex, the region associated with long-term reasoning and executive control, is not the brain's default governor in moments of stress or opportunity. The limbic system—the seat of fear, reward, and urgency—frequently overrides it. This is not a personal flaw; it is an evolutionary inheritance.

Neuroscientist Antonio Damasio's work has shown that emotions are not separate from rationality; they are integral to it. But in investing, the challenge is not emotion itself—it's *unexamined emotion.* The problem is not fear or greed per se, but how silently and swiftly they distort perception and probability.

By default, we chase gains, flee losses, and cling to control. These instincts once helped us survive predators and scarcity. Today, they compromise our ability to engage with probabilistic systems and long-term payoffs. In the markets, *emotion untrained is risk unmanaged.*

### Reflection, Not Suppression: The Art of Metacognitive Investing

Reprogramming does not mean suppressing emotion or becoming robotic. It means cultivating a metacognitive stance—a habit of thinking about how we think. It involves catching the "thought before the thought," and recognising when your decision-making is being hijacked by unexamined narratives or physiological states.

This shift is not theoretical. It is trainable. Consider the following reflective frameworks, designed for the serious investor looking to regain sovereignty over their own mind:

#### 1. The 10-10-10 Reflection

Ask:

*How will this decision feel 10 minutes from now?*

*How will I view it 10 days from now?*

*How will I judge it 10 months from now?*

This temporal distancing helps shift the investor out of emotional immediacy and into strategic perspective.

#### 2. The Bias Interruption Prompt

Before placing a trade or making an allocation, pause and ask:

*Am I acting on information or impulse?*

*What bias might be at play—confirmation, availability, loss aversion?*

*Would I make the same decision if this asset were 10% lower or higher?*

This disarms reflexive cognition and re-engages analytical clarity.

**3. The Emotional Audit**

Each week, log three market-related decisions and assign:

An emotion associated with it (e.g. anxiety, euphoria, urgency)

The context (e.g. news-driven, peer-influenced)

The outcome

Patterns emerge. Awareness compounds. Bias becomes behaviourally visible—and therefore, interruptible.

## Platforms Profit from Your Triggers—Unless You Train Against Them

One of the least discussed elements of modern investing is *interface psychology*. Most trading and investment platforms are designed for frictionless engagement—not thoughtful decision-making. Bright colours, alerts, gamification, social metrics—these are not just aesthetic choices. They are intentional stimuli engineered to drive interaction, often at the cost of discernment.

Consider Robinhood's design, which has been scrutinised for its ability to turn investing into a slot-machine experience. Or Reddit's r/WallStreetBets, which functions more as a digital colosseum of dopamine than a forum of analysis. These platforms do not cause irrationality—but they *stimulate* it.

The antidote is not avoidance but *awareness*. Investors must develop an interface hygiene—choosing tools, workflows, and environments that reinforce thoughtful engagement rather than compulsive action. This might mean:

Turning off push notifications

Using interfaces that delay order execution by design

Tracking decision rationales in a journal or dashboard

These are not technical hacks; they are psychological scaffolds.

### From Trader to Thinker: Building an Inner Investment Philosophy

The reflective investor is not simply reactive to market conditions; they are responsive to internal conditions. They do not just manage money; they manage *meaning*. This requires a clear investment philosophy—one that is coherent, adaptable, and personally aligned.

Ask:

*What does "wealth" mean to me beyond capital accumulation?*

*What trade-offs am I willing to accept in pursuit of my principles?*

*What is my posture toward uncertainty: fear, faith, or functional engagement?*

Investors who answer these questions are less likely to be blown off course by temporary volatility or algorithmic turbulence. They are playing a deeper game.

### From Reprogramming to Practice: A Model Week for the Reflective Investor

**Monday:** Review portfolio—not for performance, but for alignment. What do your current holdings say about your actual beliefs?

**Wednesday:** Block 30 minutes to write a market reflection—what patterns are you noticing in your behaviour, not just in price movements?

**Friday:** Journal one investment decision you didn't make. What stopped you? Was it wisdom or fear?

**Weekend:** Revisit a long-term goal. Is your current strategy bringing you closer or distracting you from it?

This rhythm is not rigid—it is representative. The goal is to institutionalise reflection as much as we've industrialised reaction.

### Final Thought

In a market increasingly dominated by machines, the true differentiator is not speed or scale. It is *consciousness*. Your brain is not obsolete—it is undertrained. And in a world of relentless noise and automation, *self-awareness is alpha.*

Investing will always involve uncertainty, emotion, and imperfection. But the inner investor—when cultivated—can bring to the table what no machine can: context, character, and conscious commitment. The investor who knows their mind does not need to outpace the machine. They simply need to stop being *outwitted by themselves*.

# Chapter 7
# AI-Powered Futures: Asset Classes Reimagined

There comes a point in the evolution of every advanced financial system when the foundations begin to tremble—not in the thunderous collapse of a dramatic crisis, but in a more discreet, persistent shift. The assumptions that once lent stability and coherence to markets begin to fray, sometimes imperceptibly. We are living through such a moment now. And the force at play isn't some cataclysmic economic event or a geopolitical flashpoint. It's something far more subtle—yet equally transformative: the gradual, deep-seated encroachment of artificial intelligence. Not merely as a tool, but as an agent rewriting what it means to know, to predict, and more curiously still, to define what counts as an asset.

This isn't a survey of the latest fintech fads or a prediction piece on emerging trends. Rather, it's an invitation to examine something more foundational: the very terrain of investment reality itself—and how it's being redrawn, not at the margins, but at its core. AI is no longer merely parsing the market's noise or augmenting analysts' work. It's starting to define the terms of engagement. Assets are not just being evaluated differently; they're being conceptualised through a different lens altogether—one shaped not by historical precedent but by machine reasoning.

Consider the old asset classes: equities, bonds, property, commodities—once tidy categories, each with its own metrics and expectations. Today, these distinctions are being dissolved not by their underlying value, but by how they behave as information. When an asset's meaning is increasingly mediated by how algorithms model it—its volatility, its correlations, its predictive momentum—then we're no longer operating with the same mental map. What, then, does valuation mean in a system where the data used to price risk are generated and interpreted by other machines? Are we clarifying our understanding of assets—or merely constructing more sophisticated illusions?

These questions aren't abstract. They are already influencing where capital moves, and how quickly. Take digital tokens. Their value is often a function of network dynamics interpreted by AI, not the sort of intrinsic valuation one might find in a discounted cash flow model. Or consider property markets: machine-learning platforms now pick up on microtrends invisible to human agents—shifts in noise pollution, school ratings, or tree cover—factors folded into pricing long before they appear in standard metrics. Even ESG investing, with all its ethical aspirations, is increasingly mediated by AI that scans everything from satellite imagery to social media sentiment. But what does it mean when machines take over the ethical lens?

We are, in many ways, transitioning from a world of tangible fundamentals to one dominated by synthetic inference. Investors are no longer simply responding to raw indicators. They're reacting to what AI tells them those indicators signify—and, often, to how AI predicts other machines will react. The pursuit of outperformance, once a matter of sharp analysis or insider insight, is increasingly a game of anticipating machine logic within a hall of algorithmic mirrors.

Within this evolving context, four areas stand out as bellwethers of the shift—and each, in its own way, reveals how deeply AI is remaking the logic of investment.

Start with crypto and decentralised finance. Critics are quick to dismiss it all as speculative froth, but that misses the underlying truth: DeFi is a laboratory of financial innovation. Smart contracts that execute not on fixed triggers but on probabilistic projections, liquidity pools governed by learning algorithms, decentralised insurance schemes—this isn't just a new asset class, it's a new operating system. And AI is deeply embedded, not layered on top as an afterthought.

Then, there's real estate—once the gold standard of tangible, slow-moving value. Yet here too, AI has altered the equation. Platforms now incorporate obscure data sets in real time: foot traffic, air quality, social sentiment. This isn't simply about pricing homes more accurately. It's a reinvention of how property is understood, and who gets to act on that understanding first. In such a landscape, informational asymmetry becomes not a bug, but the system's most powerful feature.

Third, the awkward but accelerating marriage between AI and ESG. Here, artificial intelligence appears to offer the rigour ESG always lacked: satellite tracking of deforestation, natural language processing to assess corporate disclosures, emotion-detection tools parsing executive interviews. But here's the sticking point—can a machine perceive motive? Can it distinguish greenwashing from genuine reform? Or does it merely reflect what can be measured, while missing what ought to matter? This isn't a technical glitch—it's a moral blind spot, and one the industry has yet to fully reckon with.

Fourth, the commodities markets. Not just the age-old barrels and bushels, but the entire class of goods whose value depends on massive, interdependent systems. Oil, grain, metals—all now priced through models that simulate not just supply and demand, but the vast mesh of factors in between: weather anomalies, political unrest, logistical bottlenecks. Here, AI isn't just offering insights—it's manufacturing the lens through which reality is seen. That shift—from grounded judgement to abstract simulation—isn't without cost.

Across all four domains, the same imperative emerges: investors can no longer rely solely on analysis; they must also become translators. The systems they engage with now speak in a blended dialect—part data science, part machine learning, part probabilistic storytelling. AI isn't simply optimising the old ways of doing things. It's constructing entirely new frameworks. Those who continue to interpret the market through a purely human lens risk falling out of sync with the tempo of change.

And yet, there's danger in the opposite extreme as well. The hazard isn't just algorithmic opacity—it's false precision. The confidence we attach to a decimal-laden machine projection often exceeds what the underlying model can genuinely support. In fact, the veneer of certainty may only deepen our collective illusions. Complexity has not eliminated ambiguity—it has, more often than not, disguised it in spreadsheets and confidence intervals. The more seductive the signal, the more vital it is to interrogate the impulse to believe it without question.

This chapter resists the urge to end with a tidy prescription. Instead, it offers a provocation: to reimagine not only where capital might be directed, but how capital itself is defined in a world where cognition is no longer exclusively human. The shape of value, the flow of markets, even the idea of what constitutes a "rational" decision—all are being recontoured in the image of intelligent systems that reflect, but do not replicate, our thinking.

William Gibson once quipped that the future is already here—it's just unevenly distributed. Nowhere is that more evident than in the world of finance. Those who grasp how AI is rewriting its rules won't merely adapt; they'll be the ones drawing the new lines on the map.

## Crypto, Tokens, and Decentralised Finance: How AI Intersects with Blockchain to Create New Investable Landscapes and Predictive Models

Money, in its most elemental form, is a ledger—a record of obligations and permissions between parties. In this light, the convergence of artificial intelligence and blockchain is not merely a technological evolution; it is a reprogramming of financial epistemology. What was once paper, later electronic, and then cryptographic, is now increasingly becoming predictive, autonomous, and decentralised. And at the heart of this evolution lies a provocative thesis: *intelligent capital is no longer solely human capital.* Today, we are witnessing the birth of self-adjusting systems that price, allocate, and distribute resources without recourse to central authorities or emotional traders. They do not sleep. They do not panic. They do not rationalise losses. They learn.

This intersection of decentralised finance (DeFi) and artificial intelligence (AI) is not speculative fiction—it is the leading edge of financial architecture. DeFi promised disintermediation, transparency, and programmable trust. AI brings pattern recognition, probabilistic forecasting, and behavioural adaptation. Together, they form a new grammar for capital markets—syntax that is automated, semantics that are dynamic, and governance that is decentralised, yet computationally rigorous.

Let us first establish what is novel here, and then probe its implications. The crypto revolution introduced smart contracts, automated market makers, non-custodial lending, and tokenised value exchange. But for all its ambition, early DeFi lacked foresight—it reacted rather than predicted. Enter AI: a layer of computational perception that can filter noise from signal, optimise transaction flows, and assess protocol risk in real-time.

Consider this: in legacy finance, risk models are often static—derived from historical volatility, mean reversion assumptions, or market beta. In DeFi, those models must cope with volatile liquidity, adversarial behaviour, and evolving tokenomics. Machine learning models are particularly suited here. They do not assume stationarity; they adapt to regime shifts, optimise yield farming strategies on the fly, and detect anomalous behaviours in pools or wallets before crises metastasise.

One early application is AI-augmented arbitrage bots. These agents do not merely scan for price disparities across decentralised exchanges—they learn which assets tend to diverge under specific liquidity conditions, predict temporary inefficiencies during governance token votes or staking events, and execute faster than any human could, often in milliseconds. What is important is not the speed per se, but the **adaptive learning**: these bots are no longer hand-coded—they are *trained.*

Beyond arbitrage, AI is being deployed to manage vault strategies in protocols like Yearn and Ribbon. These protocols optimise risk-return profiles dynamically, based on shifting market volatilities, gas fees, and strategy performance data. The machine doesn't just follow a rule—it infers the best rule to follow, continuously. In this context, **liquidity is not just capital—it is training data**.

The implications extend to decentralised governance itself. With DAOs (Decentralised Autonomous Organisations) becoming more prevalent, AI systems are being trained to model and forecast voter behaviour. Which proposals are likely to pass? Which wallets are swing votes? How will token prices respond post-vote? These questions are being answered not through intuition, but through NLP models trained on governance forums, blockchain activity, and proposal metadata.

And then there is token valuation—a realm still ruled by narrative, hype, and volatility. But AI models are increasingly being applied here too: scraping social media sentiment, tracking GitHub contributions, quantifying active addresses, and mapping token flows to assess *real* usage rather than perceived popularity. A token is no longer valued simply because "it might be the next Ethereum." It is valued because AI finds *empirical correlation* between protocol activity and market returns.

This transition also has ramifications for regulatory and ethical discourse. Predictive AI applied to blockchain data introduces a paradox: on one hand, it provides a form of surveillance capitalism inside systems designed to be permissionless. On the other, it offers a path to *risk-based compliance*—automated systems that detect wash trading, front-running, or malicious code in smart contracts before harm occurs. The line between privacy and safety, autonomy and accountability, becomes harder to draw.

Of course, this synthesis is not without its tensions. Blockchain is rooted in determinism and decentralisation. AI thrives on probabilistic inference and centralised compute. The trustless ethos of crypto can conflict with the opaque nature of machine learning models. What happens when a vault fails and no one can explain the AI's decision logic? Who is accountable when an AI-led DAO misallocates funds based on faulty training data?

This is not a philosophical sidebar—it is a governance problem, a security risk, and an ethical dilemma. Explainability, transparency, and oversight will need to evolve with these systems. Already, researchers are exploring *auditable AI*—machine learning models with built-in forensic trails and counterfactual explanations, tailored for DeFi contexts.

Meanwhile, investors—whether retail or institutional—face a new kind of due diligence. Analysing a protocol now includes assessing the robustness of its AI layer: How does it learn? What data does it use? Is it open-sourced or black-boxed? Is it susceptible to adversarial inputs or data poisoning? These are not questions about hype—they are questions about *infrastructure stability.*

And then there is the macro question: What new asset classes emerge from this fusion? We are already seeing AI-token hybrids—assets whose value is tied not to a cash flow or collateral, but to the performance of a model. Think of tokens that yield returns based on AI-generated trading signals, or insurance primitives where claim validation is executed via anomaly detection rather than human auditors.

Even stablecoins—long considered the dull backbone of crypto—are being rethought. Dynamic stablecoins, whose collateral ratios are adjusted by reinforcement learning models, are being prototyped to maintain peg more efficiently under volatile conditions. This is not just algorithmic stability—it is *adaptive resilience.*

And what of NFTs? While much maligned for speculative froth, NFTs infused with AI are giving rise to *intelligent assets*—on-chain artefacts that evolve, respond to holders, or execute behaviours algorithmically. In a DeFi context, this could mean collateral that optimises itself, or assets that represent not static value but dynamic functionality.

The boundaries between financial product and intelligent system are blurring. Capital is becoming code. Code is becoming context-aware. And context, increasingly, is learned, not programmed.

For the reader, the takeaway is not that one should blindly invest in any AI-crypto fusion. Quite the opposite. The key is discernment—understanding that this is a frontier domain with few maps, but enormous stakes. It demands both technical literacy and philosophical rigour. It demands that we ask not just *what* these systems do, but *what they are optimising for*, *who they benefit*, and *how we govern them.*

This is not the future of finance. It is already here—just unevenly distributed, often misunderstood, and rarely regulated. The intelligent investor today does not merely allocate capital. They allocate *trust* in systems. And increasingly, those systems think back.

## Real Estate in the Age of Predictive Analytics: How AI is Transforming Property Valuation, Timing, and Investment Strategy in Micro-Markets

For centuries, property investment has been the province of intuition, locality, and comparative hindsight. Success belonged to those with access—access to information, to capital, to neighbourhoods just before they gentrified. The real estate market rewarded pattern recognition, but those patterns were often drawn by the human eye: an agent's hunch, a developer's gut feeling, a financier's experience of cycles. Today, that intuition is being augmented—and in some cases outperformed—by something altogether different: machine intelligence trained not just to recognise trends, but to predict their evolution before they're visible to the human analyst.

Artificial intelligence is no longer at the periphery of real estate analytics; it is quickly becoming the foundation. And not because it replaces domain expertise, but because it reframes how we define knowledge in the property market. At its core, AI in real estate is not just about automating valuation models—it is about exposing *latent variables*, uncovering nonlinear relationships, and interpreting micro-signals that traditional econometric tools are structurally incapable of capturing.

Let us begin with valuation. Historically, the appraisal of a residential or commercial property has relied on comparable sales—"comps"—drawn from recent transactions in the surrounding area. It is a method that is simple, legible, and astonishingly fragile. Comps ignore the impact of infrastructure projects still in the planning phase. They fail to capture how noise pollution from a new highway extension might affect perceived liveability. They don't price in changing foot traffic patterns due to remote work policies. They cannot learn.

Machine learning models—particularly gradient-boosted trees and deep neural networks—can. When trained on vast arrays of structured and unstructured data, these models ingest not just price per square metre and proximity to schools, but thousands of granular features: Airbnb booking frequency, street-level crime reports, anonymised mobile device movement, even sentiment extracted from local news outlets and social media. The result is a valuation method that is contextual, adaptive, and often more predictive than traditional assessments.

And yet, valuation is only one layer. Timing—the "when" of investment—is where AI reveals its second strength. In legacy models, timing strategies are largely macro: invest counter-cyclically, look for buying opportunities in downturns, avoid bubbles. These are rules of thumb, not data-informed forecasts. AI, by contrast, allows for the modelling of *micro-cycles*—seasonal, geographic, and behavioural rhythms that are invisible to the naked eye. Consider a firm using LSTM (long short-term memory) networks to forecast short-term price movement across thousands of submarkets, or reinforcement learning agents simulating the impact of interest rate adjustments on regional real estate over time. The shift is profound:

from reactive investment strategies to proactive, scenario-driven optimisation.

A real-world illustration comes from hedge funds and institutional buyers using AI to time their entry into secondary cities—not by watching demographic averages, but by detecting pattern drift in Google search trends for job relocation, spikes in LinkedIn profile updates within a 10-mile radius, or anomalies in utility usage signalling gentrification before it hits the census data. These are not forecasts in the abstract—they are operational advantages in capital deployment.

What makes AI particularly well-suited to real estate is the spatial heterogeneity of the asset class. Every neighbourhood is a case study. Every parcel of land has unique features. It is not enough to model the market; one must model *markets within markets.* Predictive analytics tools like geospatial AI (combining satellite imagery, computer vision, and terrain classification) are being used to evaluate flood risk, proximity to natural green spaces, shadow density from nearby high-rises, and traffic flow disruptions—all of which feed directly into micro-market performance predictions. These variables are dynamic, not fixed. And AI allows investors to engage with them as fluid signals, not static checklists.

A compelling example is the integration of street-level image analysis into property scoring systems. Using machine vision, firms are now evaluating curb appeal, signage deterioration, pavement condition, and even graffiti prevalence to model community upkeep and its correlation to tenant turnover or property appreciation. Where traditional methods stopped at "number of bedrooms," these models go street by street, frame by frame.

However, with precision comes complexity. Predictive models are not oracles. They are only as robust as their training data, and they can encode blind spots if fed biased, incomplete, or improperly contextualised inputs. For example, using historical lending and appraisal data risks importing systemic biases—redlining, discrimination, or underinvestment in minority neighbourhoods. If not corrected for, these models risk perpetuating inequality under the guise of statistical sophistication.

There is also the challenge of interpretability. Black-box algorithms can outperform traditional regression models, but their opacity poses regulatory and fiduciary risks. Why did the model favour this micro-market over another? On what basis did it flag this property for high appreciation potential? Investors, particularly institutional ones, are increasingly demanding *explainable AI*—models that can articulate the weight of variables, the source of predictions, and the margin of error.

The philosophical shift here is not trivial. Real estate has always been treated as a tangible, local asset—something knowable by walking the streets, speaking with residents, visiting council planning offices. What AI challenges is the notion that proximity equals insight. It suggests that statistical distance can be more revealing than physical closeness. It moves the power of insight from geography to computation.

This has implications for retail investors too. Platforms are emerging that use AI to personalise real estate portfolios: recommending REITs, tokenised property shares, or buy-to-let opportunities based on a user's financial goals, risk profile, and even cognitive biases (e.g., whether they overvalue recency or underweight volatility). These systems are not merely responsive—they are adaptive. They observe how users respond to different asset suggestions, and evolve accordingly.

Even developers are now integrating predictive analytics into their design workflows. By simulating tenant preferences, energy consumption patterns, and future transportation access, they can optimise projects before a shovel hits the ground. AI is not just transforming where we invest—it is transforming what gets built, and for whom.

Of course, the more sophisticated these models become, the greater the temptation to defer judgment entirely to them. This is a danger. Human oversight remains indispensable—especially when models fail to capture black swan events, shifting regulatory regimes, or cultural shifts that resist quantification. Predictive analytics should augment, not replace, strategic discernment.

In summary, AI is not just another tool in the investor's kit—it is a paradigm shift in how we conceptualise, value, and act upon real estate opportunities. It is turning asset evaluation into a dynamic, data-rich science. It is recoding risk and redefining opportunity. And it is doing so across thousands of micro-markets, all synchronised not by tradition, but by inference.

For the intelligent investor, the takeaway is clear: in a world where the ground beneath our feet is increasingly mapped by machines, insight belongs to those who understand how the map is made—and how to read beyond it.

## ESG and Machine Vision: How AI Is Quantifying the Unquantifiable in Modern Investing

The investment world has long operated under a binary calculus: profit versus loss, growth versus stagnation, risk versus reward. But this ledger-based mindset no longer satisfies the modern investor—or reflects the complexity of the world in which capital now operates. Environmental, Social, and Governance (ESG) factors have moved from being non-financial niceties to core investment criteria. The challenge, however, has always been *measurement.* How does one quantify a company's carbon impact, its boardroom diversity, its supply chain ethics? Historically, these factors have been evaluated subjectively, inconsistently, and often post hoc. That is changing. Artificial intelligence—particularly in its visual and natural language processing forms—is offering a new lens through which ESG can be monitored, analysed, and actioned at scale. And in that transformation, *machine vision* has emerged as a defining tool in the effort to render the invisible, visible.

To understand the promise and provocation of this shift, it is important to first clarify the problem. ESG data has always suffered from a structural flaw: the reliance on self-reporting. Corporations issue glossy sustainability reports, pledge net-zero commitments, and offer narratives of progress. But these statements are rarely audited in real time, often omit inconvenient metrics, and are filtered through layers of public relations. Rating agencies, though improving, still rely heavily on inconsistent disclosures and static indicators. The result is a fragmented, delayed, and at times misleading picture of ESG performance.

Enter AI—not as an arbiter of morality, but as a *sensor* of reality.

Consider environmental monitoring. Satellite imagery analysed by convolutional neural networks (CNNs) is now being used to detect methane leaks, illegal deforestation, and water pollution near industrial sites—long before the companies responsible disclose such information, if they ever do. Machine vision can track the expansion of mining operations, the retreat of glaciers, or the greening of rooftops in urban centres. These aren't proxies; they're empirical observations. They shift ESG from narrative to evidence.

A notable example: one asset manager has developed a proprietary AI platform that scans daily satellite feeds to detect flaring activity at oil and gas facilities. The system flags deviations from expected emission patterns and matches these to corporate ESG disclosures. Discrepancies are noted, scored, and—where appropriate—acted upon in portfolio allocation. In short, AI doesn't just read reports; it *watches the world.*

Social factors, often considered the most nebulous in ESG analysis, are also becoming more visible under the AI lens. Computer vision, for instance, can be applied to factory footage to detect safety violations, assess worker density in unsafe conditions, or monitor for signs of forced labour in supply chains. These models, trained on annotated datasets, can flag anomalies—irregular working hours, lack of protective gear, evidence of child labour—far more effectively than human auditors conducting quarterly inspections.

And then there is governance. Traditionally the domain of board composition tables and voting records, governance now faces scrutiny from AI systems trained to parse natural language at institutional scale. Large language models (LLMs) are being fine-tuned to read meeting transcripts, earnings calls, whistleblower reports, and corporate legal filings for signs of ethical lapses, executive overreach, or strategic opacity. When analysed longitudinally, these linguistic patterns can reveal shifts in tone, confidence, or risk exposure well before they manifest in financial metrics.

But what makes these tools revolutionary is not simply the *breadth* of data they process. It is their capacity for *correlation without prejudice.* Human ESG analysts are constrained by bias, bandwidth, and framing assumptions. AI, properly trained and monitored, is indifferent to narratives. It sees what is there to be seen—no more, no less. And that impartiality is increasingly valuable in a market awash with virtue-signalling and reputational risk management.

That said, the adoption of AI in ESG brings its own tensions. One is epistemological: *What should count as evidence?* Visual confirmation of pollution may be compelling, but what about inferred behavioural risks, like underpaying subcontractors or stifling dissent in emerging markets? AI can analyse proxies—Glassdoor reviews, employee exit patterns, social media sentiment—but interpretation still requires judgment. There is a risk of *data determinism*, where only what can be measured is considered real, and what matters morally but eludes machine detection is discounted.

Another concern is opacity. Many ESG-focused AI models are proprietary and black-boxed, offering little transparency into how ratings are derived. Investors are right to be sceptical of algorithmic scores with no explanation. That is why *explainable AI* is becoming an essential design principle in the next wave of ESG analytics: not just outputting ratings, but *justifying them* in plain terms, with traceable evidence.

There are also political risks. As AI systems start flagging ESG violations automatically, companies will likely push back—claiming misinterpretation, demanding dataset audits, or lobbying regulators to standardise ESG definitions. Indeed, regulatory bodies themselves are still catching up to what is technologically possible. The EU's Sustainable Finance Disclosure Regulation (SFDR) is one step, but global ESG frameworks remain fragmented. There is little consensus, for instance, on how to weigh carbon offsets versus absolute emissions, or on how to define meaningful diversity in governance.

Despite these frictions, the trajectory is clear. Machine vision is not a panacea, but it is a profound shift. It transforms ESG from a reputational strategy into an operational dataset. It gives investors tools not just to reward good behaviour, but to detect misbehaviour early enough to act. And it aligns financial capital with *observed impact*, rather than public relations.

Importantly, this technological transformation is also cultural. It repositions ESG as something dynamic, observable, and, crucially, *real.* When investors can *see* the forest loss, *watch* the workplace conditions, and *analyse* the language of governance with machine-assisted rigour, they are more likely to treat ESG not as a checkbox, but as an investment variable with concrete implications.

For portfolio managers, this implies a shift in strategy. ESG screens can no longer be backward-looking or reliant on ratings agencies alone. Active managers must now consider satellite telemetry, sentiment models, and machine-audited supply chains as inputs in their investment process. For passive managers, the rise of real-time ESG data may lead to dynamic index rebalancing—not quarterly, but daily or hourly—based on new signals detected through AI feeds.

And for companies, the implication is existential: if you say you are green, the satellites will test that claim. If you promise equity, the language of your leaders and the structure of your board will be parsed for consistency. This is not surveillance; it is *accountability through visibility*.

In sum, ESG investing is moving from soft science to hard data. And machine vision—alongside natural language understanding and multi-modal learning—is the catalyst. We are entering a phase where the gap between a company's stated values and its observable impact can be continuously, quantitatively assessed. This is not just a shift in tools—it is a shift in power: from narrative to evidence, from promise to pattern, from spin to signal.

The responsible investor of the future will not only ask "what is this company worth?" but also "what does this company *do*—and what can we *see* to prove it?"

## Commodities and Global Risk AI: How Algorithms Are Pricing the World's Volatility

In commodity markets, price has never been a reflection of value alone—it is a signal shaped by geography, geopolitics, weather, speculation, and increasingly, algorithms. Today, a tonne of lithium, a barrel of oil, or a kilogram of cocoa carries not just the cost of extraction and transportation but the embedded probabilities of drought in Ghana, insurgency in Nigeria, political instability in Chile, and supply chain bottlenecks in the Red Sea. The variables are vast, shifting, and interconnected. Historically, the human brain—and even conventional statistical models—have struggled to synthesise this chaotic data landscape. Artificial intelligence, however, is not constrained by cognitive bandwidth or linear heuristics. It can detect non-obvious correlations, process real-time inputs from satellites and sensors, and simulate counterfactual futures faster than any human desk could. As a result, *AI is no longer just helping price commodities—it is actively reshaping how global risk is understood, mapped, and monetised.*

To appreciate the shift, we must start with the basic challenge: commodities are exposed to *exogenous volatility*. Unlike equities, where company performance can be assessed through earnings and forecasts, commodities are governed by ecosystems—climate, conflict, currency, policy—and their pricing depends on anticipating how those ecosystems interact. AI thrives in this kind of complexity, not because it simplifies the world, but because it can *model its uncertainty*.

A case in point is the way AI is transforming weather risk assessment in agriculture. Traditional crop forecasts relied on seasonal patterns and limited meteorological data. Today, machine learning models trained on decades of satellite imagery, soil moisture levels, and historical yields can make dynamic predictions about wheat production in the American Midwest, sugar in Brazil, or coffee in Vietnam. These models do not merely report conditions; they *infer yield impacts*, price sensitivities, and downstream effects across related commodities. For example, a predicted heatwave in India doesn't just affect rice futures; it changes the flow of edible oil imports, drives inflation expectations, and reconfigures fertiliser demand.

Equally transformative is AI's role in *geopolitical risk pricing*. Conflict, embargoes, regulatory shifts—these are inherently non-linear events, yet they exert disproportionate influence on oil, gas, rare earths, and metals. Natural language processing (NLP) models now scrape and interpret real-time data from diplomatic cables, news reports, intelligence leaks, and even encrypted social media platforms in regions with low press freedom. These language models are fine-tuned not just to detect overt signals—such as military deployments or sanctions announcements—but also subtle cues: tone changes in parliamentary debates, regime rhetoric, or the pacing of supply chain document filings. Traders can't afford to wait for CNN to break the story. The model gets there first.

One hedge fund has integrated this approach to track commodity-exposed regions. Their proprietary AI system assigns daily stability ratings to 85 jurisdictions based on variables such as political protests, currency movements, satellite traffic data, and deep-web chatter. This score then dynamically adjusts their exposure to copper, cobalt, and nickel—metals essential to the green energy transition but sourced largely from unstable regions like the DRC, Myanmar, and parts of South America. The fund doesn't need to guess whether a coup will happen next month; it monitors *precursor patterns* and adjusts risk positions algorithmically.

Supply chain analytics—another domain once dominated by lagging indicators—is also being redefined. Pre-AI, firms relied on customs data, port throughput, and anecdotal supplier intelligence. Now, AI platforms ingest everything from ship transponder data, procurement invoices, drone imagery, and Chinese logistics regulations, and apply graph-based models to map vulnerabilities across global networks. When a single shipping lane is disrupted—say, by a cyberattack or naval blockade—AI simulations can immediately trace cascading effects on the price of aluminium, semiconductors, or cotton. In effect, supply chain modelling has become *a live financial signal.*

However, the power of AI in commodity markets is not just about reacting faster—it's about *forecasting emergent behaviour.* Classical models are linear: if rainfall drops 10%, crop yield falls proportionally. AI models, particularly those using reinforcement learning or agent-based simulations, do not assume proportionality. They model the behaviour of market participants, producers, regulators, and speculators as *agents with competing incentives*, allowing them to simulate how a drought *plus* an export ban *plus* a speculative frenzy could trigger a price spike—or a crash.

There is also a philosophical shift underway. For decades, the commodity trader's edge was informational asymmetry. Access to insider supply data, government relationships, or regional intelligence gave firms like Glencore or Vitol their advantage. AI is democratising that edge. Now, a startup in Singapore or a sovereign wealth fund in Scandinavia can plug into satellite-based crop health analytics or NLP-based sanctions prediction tools and make allocation decisions that would have required entire research divisions a decade ago. The frontier is no longer just *what you know*, but *how well your models infer what matters*.

Yet this also introduces new forms of fragility. If too many market actors rely on similar AI-driven forecasts, *herding behaviour* becomes algorithmically reinforced. We have already seen flash crashes in equities driven by high-frequency algorithms responding to correlated signals. In commodities—where physical supply takes time to adjust—this could lead to price overreactions that amplify volatility rather than contain it. If every trader pulls out of a soy market because their AI model detected a potential trade embargo, the act of exit itself can cause price dislocation—*regardless* of whether the embargo materialises.

Moreover, AI does not eliminate uncertainty; it shifts the *types* of uncertainty we face. Model risk—the chance that the algorithm is wrong due to biased data, flawed assumptions, or adversarial manipulation—is increasingly systemic. If a climate forecasting model underestimates El Niño's impact on rainfall, and that model is embedded across institutional strategies, the resulting mispricing could be profound. AI systems are only as robust as the data and architecture that underpin them.

There are also ethical dimensions. What happens when AI models detect patterns of forced labour or environmental degradation that are financially actionable but politically inconvenient? Should hedge funds profit from early insight into humanitarian crises? Should sovereign funds be allowed to *anticipate sanctions* and reposition portfolios accordingly? As AI gives commodity traders predictive clarity, it also gives them *moral ambiguity*. What is foresight for one investor may be opportunism to another.

To reconcile this, institutional frameworks need to evolve. Model interpretability, scenario auditing, and ethical AI guidelines must become embedded within financial firms, not as compliance rituals but as investment principles. The most sophisticated asset managers are already building "model governance desks" alongside traditional trading teams—staffed not just with data scientists, but also ethicists and geopolitical analysts who interrogate what the model sees, and *why* it sees it.

Looking ahead, commodity pricing will likely move towards *multi-layered models*: hybrid systems that combine physical data (satellites, sensors, shipping records), human judgment (local analysts, domain experts), and AI inference engines trained on decades of market memory. These systems will not just forecast price—they will simulate regimes of volatility, model confidence intervals of disruption, and recalibrate exposure in near real-time.

The implications extend beyond finance. Governments, NGOs, and disaster response teams are beginning to leverage these same tools for resilience planning. If an AI model can predict a rice shortfall in Southeast Asia six months in advance, that's not just a trade signal—it's a food security alert. If it can detect warming ocean currents and forecast fish migration patterns, it can inform sustainable quotas. The same tools that price risk can, if directed with care, *help mitigate it.*

The bottom line is this: commodities are no longer priced purely on supply and demand—they are priced on *systems intelligence.* AI has become the nerve centre of that intelligence, connecting weather to war, policy to pricing, and scarcity to speculation. For investors, that means opportunity—but also responsibility. Because when your model sees the storm before it hits, the question is no longer *what will you do with that insight?* It's *who else will feel its impact?*

# Chapter 8
# Philosophy of Risk in an Automated Age

We are living through a time when machines—not minds—are beginning to chart the outer edges of financial danger. In mere microseconds, algorithms process torrents of market signals, spit out probability curves, and execute trades worth millions. Hedge funds now sculpt their portfolios through Monte Carlo simulations. Deep-learning networks scan weather anomalies to predict shifts in agricultural commodities. Insurance premiums rise or fall thanks to reinforcement learning systems that sift through far more data than any human actuary could ever hope to grasp. And yet, for all this technological bravura, something essential has been left behind: our philosophical understanding of risk. We've conflated risk with volatility, mistaken precision for control, and allowed models to stand in for the messy, unknowable nature of reality. The result? A slow but troubling slide into a kind of automated naivety. This chapter sets out to dismantle that illusion—piece by flawed piece.

Treating risk as a tidy beta coefficient or a clean bell curve might work well enough for spreadsheets. But as a way to navigate genuine uncertainty? It's woefully inadequate. Risk, at its core, isn't about fluctuation; it's about consequence. Not just how likely a loss is, but how deep, how lasting. A volatile tech share jumping daily might pose less of a threat than a once-in-a-generation failure of an AI system controlling energy pricing for a nation. The real peril comes when investors blur the line between instability and irreversibility—mistaking sophistication for safety and gambling with something they don't fully understand.

Consider a high-frequency trading desk, powered by a machine-learning engine designed to exploit momentary pricing inefficiencies. Everything ticks along perfectly—until it doesn't. Imagine it wandering into an uncharted configuration of market events: a geopolitical shock, a flash liquidity freeze, and a cascade of trades it was never trained to anticipate. The algorithm doesn't err by flailing randomly. No, it does exactly what it was programmed to do—only in a context its creators hadn't imagined. This isn't simply volatility.

It's epistemic fragility—failure not in the known unknowns, but in the terrain we never thought to map.

So let's start here: risk isn't merely a statistical remnant. It's a condition of being. And in systems increasingly governed by artificial intelligence, that truth becomes harder to ignore. When we delegate choices to algorithms, we don't eliminate bias—we displace it. The models still carry human fingerprints: in their training data, their reward functions, their assumptions—often implicit, occasionally flawed. The more seamless the output, the easier it is to forget what lies beneath. Progress can, in fact, be a new kind of opacity. Risk hasn't vanished. It's just been given a more palatable disguise.

Then there's the matter of temperament. People often dramatically overestimate how much uncertainty they can actually live with. Serene markets get mistaken for inner calm. Behavioural economists have highlighted these misjudgements for decades—loss aversion, overconfidence, the halo effect. The entrance of AI into portfolio design only heightens this disconnection. Robo-advisors present clean graphs and frictionless rebalancing. What they rarely do is provoke an honest reckoning: how will this investor actually feel when the loss is no longer hypothetical, but painfully real? That 10% drawdown might seem abstract on paper—until it's threatening your child's tuition or your own livelihood. The arithmetic may be impeccable. The emotional toll? Often left out of the equation.

This chapter pushes for a more grounded self-assessment. Not just "How much risk am I willing to take?" but "How much can I really afford to endure?" The distinction is subtle, but critical. A sound investor isn't one who has memorised risk metrics, but one who's mapped those abstractions to their own lived responsibilities. How long can I remain exposed before I imperil something I hold dear? Where do my principles draw the line—between return and ethics, between ambition and prudence? These aren't questions you pose to a model. They belong to an older, more introspective discipline: judgment.

It's here we must tip our hats to thinkers like Nassim Nicholas Taleb. His Black Swan theory—a reminder that the most impactful events are often unimaginable before they strike—sits as a necessary rejoinder to the statistical confidence of modern finance. AI thrives on patterns it recognises. What it doesn't do—what it can't do—is perceive the patterns it hasn't seen. The greatest shocks, by definition, sit outside the model's gaze. This isn't a flaw to patch—it's a limitation we must accept. As Taleb wryly notes, we build our systems as though we understand the future, then act surprised when it fails to arrive on cue. We don't need to abandon models, but we do need to temper them—with humility, and with memory.

None of this should be read as an invitation to retreat into cynicism. Quite the opposite. This chapter outlines the scaffolding for a more thoughtful risk philosophy—one that values data without becoming enslaved by it. We ask what it might look like to construct frameworks that honour not only return targets but broader goals: legacy, stewardship, meaning. It's not merely a question of "Which risks are worth taking?" but "Which ones are worth bearing?" What turbulence can I live through without compromising who I am? Which decisions, though safe on a spreadsheet, would still keep me up at night?

Time itself needs rethinking. Machines operate in milliseconds. Human lives unfold over decades. Risk management, then, isn't about micromanaging loss—it's about constructing a life that can hold up under vastly uneven tempos. The 28-year-old with compounding on their side plays a different game than the 68-year-old budgeting for longevity. Yet so many risk profiles freeze these distinctions into a single, static number. They ignore the evolving nature of what matters to us, and when. This chapter argues for something more adaptive: a framework that moves as we do, that shifts not with market flickers, but with the long arc of personal change.

Towards the end, we explore some of the more emergent, intellectually rich approaches to risk—tools like regret minimisation, inverse utility modelling, probabilistic satisficing. These aren't silver bullets, but they are serious attempts to blend the precision of finance with the messiness of human life. They recognise that clarity is often partial, and that wisdom sometimes lies not in optimising for the best outcome, but in avoiding the ones we couldn't live with.

In the end, this chapter does not seek to tame risk or strip it of its sting. Rather, it tries to see it more honestly. It challenges the illusion of algorithmic omniscience and calls for a posture of alertness—not fear, but discernment. Because risk, in the final account, isn't what the model spits out. It's what you're prepared to shoulder, and what you're unwilling to sacrifice, when the future comes knocking uninvited.

## What Is Risk, Really?

*A philosophical interrogation of risk—not as volatility, but as consequence, irreversibility, and personal cost*

If you ask a fund manager, a fintech platform, and a behavioural psychologist to define risk, you will likely get three different answers—none of them wrong, but few of them complete. In most financial contexts, risk is defined by volatility: a quantifiable range of potential outcomes, typically measured by statistical deviation from the mean. But this conception, while useful for portfolio theory, fails to account for the real-life gravity of decision-making under uncertainty. Risk is not simply movement on a chart. It is *exposure to consequences that matter*—to outcomes that could irreversibly change one's financial, emotional, or ethical standing in the world. In this deeper sense, risk is not a number. *It is a narrative.*

This chapter asks you to reconsider risk at its root. Not as a metric, but as a philosophical and human phenomenon. We're not discussing how to optimise a Sharpe ratio—we're examining what it means to act under incomplete information, with finite resilience, and with skin in the game. When machines model volatility, they offer abstraction. But when people make choices, they feel *irreversibility.* This distinction—between statistical probability and existential exposure—is the foundation of a more truthful, more resilient risk philosophy.

### Volatility Is Not Vulnerability

Let's begin with the most common mischaracterisation: equating risk with volatility. In finance, volatility reflects the degree of variation in asset prices over time. It's a neutral measure—stocks can swing wildly upward as easily as downward. But for most people, the idea of "risk" intuitively includes the potential for *harm*. That's why a stable investment in a morally dubious venture might carry little volatility but *immense reputational or psychological risk*. Conversely, an asset with high volatility but robust fundamentals might offer little true risk if the holder has time, liquidity, and clarity of purpose.

This disconnect isn't just semantic—it's strategic. Over-reliance on volatility as a proxy for risk leads to dangerous underestimations of what philosopher Nassim Nicholas Taleb calls "tail events"—the rare, high-impact outcomes that define careers, collapse funds, and upend economies. These Black Swan events may fall far outside the bell curve, but they carry disproportionate weight. The 2008 financial crisis was not "risky" by standard deviation the year before it occurred. Nor was the COVID-19 pandemic priced into most risk models in late 2019. Yet both reshaped global markets. Why? Because *real risk lives in the fat tails of consequence, not in the tidy confidence intervals of convenience.*

### Risk as Irreversibility

The next axis of risk that traditional models overlook is *irreversibility*. A reversible decision is not truly risky—it's experimental. You can iterate, revert, or pause. But in investing, many decisions are not so forgiving. Liquidating long-held assets in a downturn, withdrawing retirement funds prematurely, or leveraging at the wrong moment are all actions with compounding consequences. The damage, once done, is not just financial. It's emotional. It often changes behaviour permanently, narrowing future optionality.

Consider a young investor who panic-sells during a market correction, locks in a loss, and misses the rebound. The technical risk—the market volatility—may have been temporary. But the *personal risk* was enduring: a shaken confidence in investing that leads to long-term underexposure to growth assets. What was lost wasn't just capital—it was *trust in the system*, in oneself, and in the notion of recovery. A better framework, then, treats risk not as fluctuation, but as *path dependency*: the extent to which a wrong step can foreclose future steps entirely.

## The Personal Cost of Probability

This leads us to perhaps the most underappreciated element of risk: its *personal cost*. Too often, investment platforms present probabilities in abstract terms, divorced from real-life context. "There's a 70% chance this asset will rise over the next 12 months." That sounds comforting—until you realise that 30% of the time, it won't. And if your financial life cannot absorb that outcome—if it would derail your plans, disrupt your family, or violate your values—then that 30% is not a tolerable minority. *It's a deal-breaker.*

The same logic applies at the institutional level. A hedge fund might model a 1% chance of catastrophic loss and consider it acceptable. But if that 1% corresponds to a scenario where global liquidity freezes or investor confidence evaporates, then the real risk is not the likelihood—it's the *irreversibility* of the fallout. AI models often fail to make this distinction. They are trained on historical data. They know what has happened. They do not know what could *matter* in the future.

## Measuring What Models Miss

AI-driven investing platforms today can digest vast amounts of data: satellite imagery, ESG reports, social sentiment, macro indicators. They are more precise than any human analyst. But they are also more detached. They do not possess *perspective*. They do not weigh ethical dilemmas, career-defining reputational costs, or the slow erosion of public trust. Nor do they feel the pain of real investors watching their savings evaporate in a liquidity event. This is not a limitation of technology—it is a philosophical vacuum.

An AI model can tell you which assets are correlated, how earnings surprises affect short-term prices, and which macro scenarios are most likely to unfold. But it cannot tell you whether the risks you are taking *fit your life*. That is a human question. One that requires *self-awareness, scenario planning, and moral clarity*—not just predictive power.

## Rethinking Risk Tolerance

Most platforms ask new investors to take a "risk profile" survey. These typically gauge how comfortable you are with seeing your portfolio drop by certain percentages. But such framing confuses hypothetical comfort with *lived capacity*. The better question is not "Can you tolerate a 20% drop?" but "What are the consequences if this drop happens at the wrong time, for the wrong reasons, with no clear recovery in sight?" True risk tolerance is not about bravado. It is about *resilience under imperfect conditions*.

To build this resilience, investors must interrogate not only their goals, but their constraints: What obligations must be protected at all costs? What timelines are immovable? What moral or personal lines are not worth crossing for incremental return? These are not data points. They are *value statements*. And they should shape every definition of risk worth taking seriously.

## Toward a More Complete Philosophy of Risk

To understand risk deeply is to see beyond markets. It is to recognise that every decision is a bet—not just on financial outcomes, but on *narratives, values, and consequences*. Sometimes, the riskiest move is doing nothing. Other times, it's acting on models without context. As AI expands its role in portfolio construction and real-time pricing, the burden of wisdom shifts. Machines can optimise based on precedent. But humans must decide what they are optimising *for*.

The philosopher Søren Kierkegaard once wrote that life must be lived forward, but can only be understood backward. Risk, in this light, is not merely about foresight—it's about *integrity in the face of uncertainty*. You cannot know everything. But you can know *what matters most*, and you can protect against irreversibility in those domains.

This subchapter offers a framework for doing just that. It replaces the shallow language of probability with the deeper grammar of consequence. It challenges the reader to build not just a portfolio, but a worldview resilient to ambiguity. Because at the end of the day, investing is not about avoiding risk. It's about *recognising which risks are worth taking—and which will never be worth the cost.*

## Risk Tolerance vs. Risk Illusion

*Helping readers redefine their own comfort with uncertainty through psychological and strategic lenses*

There is a quiet but consequential assumption embedded into most modern investing tools: that individuals can accurately assess their tolerance for risk. It's a premise baked into investor onboarding surveys, asset allocation algorithms, and robo-advisory models. You are asked how you feel about hypothetical market declines—if you could stomach a 20% drop, whether you'd rebalance or retreat, how you might react under financial pressure. And based on your answers, a risk profile is generated. Clean, efficient, scientific.

But it's a fiction.

What most of these models capture is not *actual risk tolerance*—the capacity to endure real loss or uncertainty—but *risk illusion*: a fragile and often false sense of comfort with volatility under artificial, decontextualised conditions. People are terrible at predicting how they'll behave under stress. Even seasoned professionals fall prey to this cognitive blind spot, overestimating their resilience and underestimating the gravity of unknowns. This subchapter is about replacing that illusion with a more honest, flexible, and grounded understanding of risk—one that can hold up under pressure.

### Why the Concept of "Tolerance" Misleads

The term *risk tolerance* implies a stable, measurable trait—like height or blood pressure. But in reality, risk preferences fluctuate. They are *context-sensitive*, *emotion-dependent*, and deeply affected by framing. A person may claim they're comfortable with a volatile asset class during a bull market, only to panic-sell when markets correct sharply. Similarly, a self-declared conservative investor might suddenly chase speculative returns during a period of FOMO-fuelled euphoria.

This instability is not irrational; it is *human*. Behavioural finance research, particularly by scholars like Daniel Kahneman and Amos Tversky, has repeatedly shown that people are *loss averse*—the psychological pain of losing is significantly more potent than the pleasure of gaining. Yet we rarely account for that disparity when estimating our risk preferences. Theoretical comfort with uncertainty often evaporates in the face of actual loss, particularly when coupled with the emotional triggers of media panic, social comparison, or deadline-induced decision-making.

In other words, *the conditions under which risk tolerance is tested are never the same as those under which it is declared.*

### Simulation vs. Reality: A Critical Gap

Investor risk surveys and profiling tools are attempts to simulate real-world decision-making. But simulations are inherently limited by *what they can model.* They typically ask individuals to respond to numerical prompts: "How would you react to a 10% drop in your portfolio?" or "Would you sell, hold, or buy more?" These prompts treat risk as an *intellectual abstraction*, rather than an *embodied experience.*

This is problematic for two reasons:

1. Most people process risk *emotionally*, not mathematically.

2. The actual experience of risk is *temporal and narrative-based*—it unfolds over time, with uncertainty, and without resolution in advance.

You don't *know* how you'll feel about a drawdown until you're in one. And when you're in it, you're not responding to a clean number—you're reacting to a complex narrative: market headlines, peer behaviour, family concerns, and your own internal dialogue. As such, *risk is not just about probability—it's about perceived consequence.*

### The Psychology of Illusion: Anchors, Biases, and False Certainties

Psychologists have identified numerous cognitive biases that distort how we perceive risk. Anchoring is one of the most powerful. When an investor hears that the average return of the S&P 500 is around 10% annually, they mentally "anchor" to that number, expecting future outcomes to gravitate around it—even though actual returns vary dramatically year to year.

Another common distortion is *availability bias*: the tendency to overestimate the likelihood of events that are more memorable or emotionally vivid. For example, a recent crash or market crisis will loom disproportionately large in an investor's psyche, leading them to perceive far greater risk than data would justify. Conversely, during long bull markets, *recency bias* creates a dangerous illusion of safety—people confuse trend persistence with systemic stability.

The consequence is a kind of dual miscalibration: *underestimating risk when it's growing quietly in the background, and overestimating it when it finally erupts.* Both errors are driven not by ignorance, but by *narrative coherence*: the brain's need to make uncertainty feel digestible, even when it is not.

### Strategic Clarity vs. Emotional Certainty

To move beyond the illusion of risk tolerance, we must shift from an emotional to a strategic posture. That doesn't mean suppressing emotion—it means building a *risk philosophy* that anticipates emotional disruption and mitigates its effects.

This involves several key pivots:

**From comfort to consequence**: Don't ask "Can I tolerate this loss?" Ask "What happens to my life if this loss occurs?"

**From forecasts to flex points**: Assume uncertainty, not control. Create plans that don't require you to predict outcomes accurately but allow you to adapt wisely.

**From static profiles to dynamic readiness**: Treat your risk capacity as evolving. Periodically review it against changes in your income, goals, dependents, health, and worldview.

**From numerical targeting to narrative integrity**: Align investment decisions not just with risk-reward ratios but with your *story of self*—your sense of who you are and what you value most when tested.

These shifts reposition risk as a dialogue between *data and dignity*—between what the models say is statistically safe and what *you know is meaningful.*

**A Case in Contrast: The Tech Worker and the Property Investor**

Consider two investors: one is a 30-year-old software engineer with a high salary, no dependents, and a strong belief in the future of decentralised finance. The other is a 55-year-old property investor with two children nearing university and an ill spouse.

Traditional risk profiling might place both somewhere in the "moderate" bracket due to their net worth. But their *actual exposure to risk* could not be more different. The engineer has time, income fluidity, and appetite for experimentation. The property investor has immovable obligations, liquidity constraints, and a low margin for error.

Yet in a rising market, both might take similar positions—driven not by strategic alignment, but by the psychological illusion that because they've done well recently, they *can afford to be bold.* This is how risk illusions form: *not in spreadsheets, but in streaks*—a string of good outcomes misread as a signal of skill or stability.

### Toward an Adaptive Risk Framework

If we accept that true risk tolerance is contextual, dynamic, and often invisible until tested, then we need tools that reflect that complexity. Not static surveys, but reflective frameworks. Below are examples of questions that offer deeper insight:

*Which losses would I consider inconvenient, and which would I consider unacceptable?*

*What are the obligations I cannot fail to meet, regardless of market conditions?*

*What patterns do I notice in my past decisions under pressure—do I freeze, retreat, overcompensate?*

*Which voices (media, friends, advisors) disproportionately influence my perception of risk, and why?*

*How do I want to behave in a crisis—and what systems will help me do so?*

These are not checkboxes. They are *compass points.* And over time, they can recalibrate the illusion of confidence into the substance of clarity.

### The Role of AI: Model-Assisted, Not Model-Determined

AI systems have become increasingly sophisticated at quantifying market risk, building predictive models, and even adjusting portfolios in real time. But they still lack an understanding of *personal consequence.* An algorithm can recommend risk exposure based on age and income, but it cannot model your fear of losing a home, your hope of retiring early to care for ageing parents, or your desire to fund a social cause.

That's why the goal is not to eliminate emotion from investment decisions—it's to *educate emotion with structure*, to pair behavioural self-awareness with machine intelligence. AI can provide adaptive guardrails, but *only you can decide which cliffs are worth approaching.*

**Final Thought: From False Comfort to Constructive Discomfort**

Ultimately, redefining risk tolerance is not about finding the perfect portfolio. It's about replacing the *illusion of stability* with the *capacity for response.* You won't eliminate risk. But you can build the self-awareness, strategic clarity, and emotional maturity to face it on terms you've chosen—rather than ones you've absorbed unknowingly.

The next time you're asked how much risk you're willing to take, pause. Consider not just the metric, but the meaning. Because true tolerance isn't about having the stomach for volatility. *It's about having the spine for consequence.*

## Living with the Unknowable

*Why Even AI Cannot Map What It Cannot Conceive*

On a bright morning in 2008, Lehman Brothers filed for bankruptcy. The global economy, seemingly stable only weeks before, began to fracture with astonishing speed. Analysts scrambled, models failed, and central banks braced against a tide they hadn't forecast. Retrospective explanations came quickly—subprime contagion, leverage excess, regulatory blindness—but in real time, most were caught entirely off guard. It was not the volatility that made the moment historic. It was the *shock*. The inability to see it coming.

This, at its core, is the problem of the *unknowable*—a category of uncertainty that escapes both statistical probability and narrative intuition. Nassim Nicholas Taleb gave this phenomenon its now-familiar name: the *Black Swan.* Not simply rare, but *unimaginable until after the fact*, Black Swans fracture our maps of causality. They also challenge a key assumption behind modern investing and predictive AI alike: that more data, processed faster, will lead to clearer foresight.

It won't.

### The Black Swan Defined—And Misunderstood

Taleb's formulation was not merely that improbable events occur, but that we consistently underestimate their frequency and impact due to structural blind spots in how we think about risk. We tend to confuse the absence of evidence for evidence of absence. If no war, crash, or pandemic has occurred recently, we presume a lower likelihood of one occurring tomorrow. But this is a form of *inductive complacency*, not probability. And this error is precisely what Black Swans exploit.

Most critically, Black Swans *cannot be predicted by historical data.* They are not tail events in a standard Gaussian distribution. They are *unknown unknowns*—emerging from domains we haven't modelled, assumptions we haven't questioned, or interconnections we haven't noticed. That renders them fundamentally incompatible with traditional forecasting.

And herein lies the philosophical rub: even with infinite data, a system cannot anticipate that which falls outside its model's architecture. This isn't a software issue. It's a *conceptual* boundary.

### Why AI Still Fails at Radical Uncertainty

Today, machine learning systems process more financial information in a second than any human could in a lifetime. They forecast market trends, identify pricing anomalies, and detect subtle patterns across datasets with ruthless efficiency. But this processing power should not be mistaken for omniscience.

AI excels at *interpolation*—identifying relationships within a known dataset—but struggles with *extrapolation*, particularly when those extrapolations enter domains where the rules change or where the model's assumptions are invalidated. No AI trained on pre-2007 financial data would have *imagined* the systemic interlinkages that brought down the banking sector. No pandemic-prediction algorithm flagged Wuhan with confident clarity in late 2019.

This is not a failure of optimisation. It is a consequence of *model-dependent blindness.* AI systems, especially deep learning ones, are only as robust as their training environments. They do not have "imagination" in the human sense. They cannot contemplate events outside of their encoded domain logic. And so, when real-world systems evolve—when politics destabilise markets, when a bioterror event distorts oil prices, or when a social contagion triggers asset sell-offs—AI is, often, as surprised as we are.

*More data will not rescue a model from a flawed premise.*

### The Comfort of Control—And the Illusion It Brings

Much of modern finance rests on the premise that risk can be managed—priced, transferred, hedged. It's a comforting narrative, and to an extent, it's true. But only within a certain spectrum. When investors or institutions begin to confuse *measurable volatility* with *true risk*, they slide into a dangerous epistemic zone: what philosopher David Hume might call the tyranny of precedent.

Historical data is not a map of the future. It's a record of *what happened under specific conditions.* If the conditions change, the record misleads.

This creates an illusion of control. The tighter we bind our strategies to high-confidence data correlations, the more exposed we may become to regime shifts, policy discontinuities, or moral panic—none of which fit within a tidy quantitative schema. Taleb's critique of financial orthodoxy was not anti-quantitative per se, but anti-naïve—an insistence that models cannot capture the full spectrum of causal dynamics in a nonlinear world.

## Strategic Implications: Embracing Robustness Over Precision

So how should thoughtful investors—or AI designers—respond? The answer lies not in discarding models, but in *reconceptualising their purpose*. If prediction is limited, then *resilience* becomes primary. The goal shifts from attempting to foresee every outcome to designing systems that can *withstand* and *adapt to* the ones we fail to see.

This logic underpins Taleb's advocacy for "antifragility"—a term describing systems that *benefit from disorder*. Such systems avoid over-optimised efficiency (which tends to be brittle) in favour of redundancy, decentralisation, and optionality. Think of how venture capital portfolios operate: most startups fail, but the few that succeed do so massively, more than offsetting the losses. That's not diversification—it's *asymmetry* by design.

In contrast, many AI-driven quant strategies today are razor-thin in margin and hyper-leveraged in exposure. They perform beautifully in calm waters and break spectacularly during storms. What's needed is not just more intelligence, but *philosophical humility*. A shift from the illusion of mastery toward the architecture of survivability.

## Black Swans in the Wild—A Post-2020 Reminder

If Taleb's theories once seemed abstract, the COVID-19 pandemic should have erased any remaining doubt. In a world supposedly ruled by real-time data and predictive models, most governments, businesses, and markets were caught unprepared. Supply chains snapped, oil went negative, and volatility indices spiked to 80+. AI systems scrambled to recalibrate, but they had no precedent for a global shutdown layered with misinformation, political instability, and asynchronous reopening.

The same principle applied during the early weeks of Russia's invasion of Ukraine, when commodity prices whipsawed unpredictably, or when the collapse of Silicon Valley Bank in 2023 sent tremors through asset-backed debt instruments that had looked pristine on paper.

Each of these events was knowable *in theory*, yet invisible *in practice.* Why? Because the systems charged with anticipating them were optimised for *expected variation*, not *discontinuous emergence.* They could project trends, but not paradigm shifts.

## Living with the Unknowable: A Mental Model

To navigate a world of Black Swans, we must adopt a mindset that combines *strategic humility* with *dynamic optionality*. This does not mean fearing every shadow. It means acknowledging that the future is not just unknown, but partially *unknowable*, and thus requires a posture of *adaptive readiness* rather than static certainty.

Ask not: "What is most likely to happen?"
Ask instead: "What would break me if it did happen—and how can I design to survive it?"

This inversion of risk logic moves the focus from probabilities to *consequences.* It also forces a reevaluation of the kind of intelligence we value—not just data-crunching power, but interpretive awareness, scenario range, and the capacity for second-order thinking.

## Final Thought: The Limits of Prediction Are Not the Limits of Insight

AI is changing investing. But it is not *solving* investing. Nor is it capable of abolishing uncertainty, no matter how refined the algorithms. What it can do—brilliantly—is augment our vision, accelerate pattern recognition, and surface latent correlations. What it cannot do is render risk obsolete.

Understanding Black Swans is not a call for cynicism. It's a call for *intellectual maturity.* A reminder that wisdom often lies not in more confident forecasts, but in better questions—and more durable frameworks.

The future is not a formula. It is a fragile, turbulent landscape of partial knowledge, subjective narratives, and unseen dynamics. Any strategy that forgets this, no matter how advanced, is not insight—it is hubris in code.

## Redesigning Your Risk Philosophy

The notion of risk, in modern finance, often wears the borrowed language of volatility and standard deviation. But real risk—the kind that shatters retirement plans, erodes sleep, or provokes a career-altering decision—rarely announces itself as a statistical artefact. It arrives in the form of irreversible consequence. It's not about how often you're wrong, but how badly. In this light, any serious conversation about risk cannot remain confined to charts, Sharpe ratios, or Gaussian assumptions. It must expand to include values, vulnerability, and one's evolving relationship with uncertainty.

This chapter invites the reader to not only quantify risk but *philosophise* it. Because risk, at its core, is not a market feature. It is a *human interpretation* of exposure to harm. And no algorithm—no matter how sophisticated—can fully internalise what you alone are positioned to lose. The goal here is not simply to be more "rational" about risk, but more *honest*, more *aware*, and more *deliberate*. To architect a personalised philosophy of risk that transcends spreadsheets and anchors itself in your lived reality.

### Risk Is Personal, Not Universal

The modern investor is surrounded by risk metrics: Value at Risk, beta, downside deviation. But rarely do these abstractions prompt reflection on what risk *feels like* to the individual—emotionally, psychologically, or ethically. A leveraged position in a volatile asset may be mathematically "optimal" for a hedge fund manager but catastrophic for a new parent. Two investors may hold identical portfolios and inhabit completely different levels of existential risk.

This divergence is not a flaw of analysis; it is a blind spot of over-reliance on impersonal frameworks. The real opportunity lies in reframing risk as something deeply *contextual.* Your career stage, family obligations, emotional temperament, and ethical red lines all modulate how you experience exposure. Designing a personal risk philosophy demands an inventory of what matters to you *beyond* the balance sheet.

## The Problem with Borrowed Convictions

Investors frequently outsource their risk philosophy—whether by following a model portfolio, mimicking a high-profile manager, or chasing the comfort of historical averages. This is not mere laziness; it's a byproduct of the overwhelming complexity of modern markets. But the illusion of certainty borrowed from someone else's framework does not immunise you from personal consequences. Risk conviction that isn't self-derived is a liability disguised as sophistication.

One of the most important shifts an investor can make is from *imitation to introspection.* Asking, not "what would Warren Buffett do?", but rather "what outcome can I *live with* if I'm wrong?" This subtle reorientation changes everything. It transforms risk from an external threat to an internal alignment problem.

## Data Cannot Substitute for Values

In an age of machine learning and high-frequency data, it's tempting to believe that the problem of risk can be "solved" through better modelling. And yes, data can illuminate. It can refine probabilities, reveal correlations, and model tail events with increasing elegance. But risk is not just about likelihood. It's about *tolerance for consequence*—something no neural network can meaningfully assess on your behalf.

Moreover, the future is not a simulation. When a portfolio crashes during a geopolitical crisis or an environmental catastrophe, it is not the prediction that will save the investor—it is their *prior preparation.* Resilience does not come from foresight alone. It comes from clarity of values. If you do not know *what you're willing to risk and why*, then no amount of forecasting will protect you from your own unexamined exposure.

### Exercises in Recalibrating Risk

Redesigning your risk philosophy is not a one-off intellectual exercise—it's an ongoing calibration of identity, values, and environment. Here are three foundational practices that shift risk thinking from reactive to reflective:

### 1. Conduct a Consequence Inventory

List the ten worst-case scenarios—not in terms of probability, but in terms of *impact.* Ask: What would permanently alter my quality of life or sense of security? Now, map your current financial exposures against that list. You may find that you are tolerating risks you would never *consciously* accept if you saw them clearly.

### 2. Perform a Regret Simulation

Imagine that your current strategy fails catastrophically. Then ask: Would I regret *the outcome*—or the *decision-making process* that led there? If the latter, your philosophy needs work. A sound risk strategy is not one that guarantees positive results; it's one that leaves your dignity intact even when events don't go your way.

### 3. Align with a Personal Ethic

Define your "ethical stop-loss"—not just how much capital you're willing to lose, but *what behaviours or trades would violate your principles* even if they were profitable. Risk that betrays your moral compass will eventually exact a psychological toll, regardless of ROI.

These exercises aren't about insulating yourself from failure—they're about building a risk profile that *withstands* failure without collapse.

### The Myth of the Optimal Portfolio

Many investors still seek the "optimal" risk-return trade-off. But optimality is often a mirage—a construct that only holds under unrealistic assumptions: infinite time horizons, stable correlations, frictionless markets. A personal risk philosophy does not chase perfection; it seeks *coherence* between one's aspirations, vulnerabilities, and decision-making under pressure.

Sometimes the better portfolio is not the one with the highest Sharpe ratio but the one you can *hold onto* when the world turns upside down. This is where behavioural finance intersects with philosophy: the best strategy is the one that is both intellectually sound and emotionally survivable.

### Building Resilience, Not Just Efficiency

Traditional risk management systems emphasise *efficiency*: diversification, rebalancing, statistical guardrails. But a truly evolved risk philosophy shifts focus to *resilience*. That means designing systems—both internal and external—that can endure the unexpected without unravelling.

Resilience asks different questions than efficiency:

What part of my portfolio can absorb a hit without panic?

Which assets or strategies increase optionality under uncertainty?

What non-financial supports (social capital, health, adaptability) buttress my financial decision-making?

Resilience assumes the future will *surprise you*. It prepares not through precision, but through adaptability.

### Redefining Success in Risk Terms

Success is often misdefined in purely financial terms—returns, alpha, benchmarks beaten. A deeper metric of success might be this: *How much of your risk was consciously chosen, internally aligned, and sustainably borne?* If your wins are built on anxiety, misalignment, or borrowed conviction, then even a profitable strategy may be hollow.

Conversely, a strategy that earns modest returns but is anchored in clarity, dignity, and purpose may offer the kind of compounded advantage that transcends numbers.

Markets are becoming more automated, more efficient, more intelligent. But your *risk philosophy* cannot be outsourced to an algorithm. It must be built, tested, revised—by you. Because risk, ultimately, is not about the system. It's about *your* exposure, *your* decisions, and *your* ability to carry the weight of the unknown with both intelligence and integrity.

To redesign your risk philosophy is to accept that uncertainty is not a problem to be solved but a reality to be inhabited. And that wisdom in risk does not lie in outsmarting chaos, but in living through it—anchored by a compass of your own design.

# Chapter 9
# Building Your AI-Enhanced Investment Philosophy

Most investors, truth be told, never quite slow down long enough to forge a philosophy of their own. They collect tools like magpies—grabbing hold of stray opinions, market commentary, back-tested models—always in pursuit of returns, with the quiet, unspoken hope that diversification will shield them from what they don't quite understand. There's a lot of hedging, most of it instinctive; plenty of signal-reading, often reactive; and yes, occasional luck, dressed up later as acumen. But what's missing—almost systematically—is any sustained questioning of the logic behind their actions. No examination of the frameworks they default to under pressure. Little awareness of the values, or even assumptions, that quietly guide their hand. The result? Portfolios stitched together from second-hand ideas: strategy without spine, tactics detached from intent, and risk undertaken with neither clarity nor inner reckoning. In an era increasingly governed by machine-driven decision-making, this absence of philosophical grounding has shifted from a forgivable oversight to a critical flaw.

This chapter doesn't concern itself with code. Nor is it preoccupied with the usual fanfare around automation, or the lure of whatever sleek new alpha-hunting device has just come onto the scene. What matters here runs deeper. We're speaking now of mental architecture—the scaffolding of conviction that holds your decision-making together when markets sway and moods fray. A genuine investment philosophy isn't some abstract exercise. It's ballast. It stabilises. It lends proportion and coherence to your choices—through the frenzy of a bull run or the fog of a drawdown, across cycles of innovation and waves of personal doubt. And now, with artificial intelligence no longer on the horizon but already in the cockpit, building that foundation is no longer optional. It's imperative.

For AI does not, despite the optimism of some, resolve the core human tension of investing. It reshapes it, heightens it, and—if we're not careful—exploits it. Yes, it offers remarkable capabilities: uncanny prediction, hyper-tailored optimisation, eerily precise personalisation. But with that power comes a fresh crop of dangers. Chief among them: the allure of mistaking noise for signal, of divorcing models from economic reality, of handing over not just your processes but—more dangerously—your judgement. Let's not delude ourselves: if you aren't clear on your beliefs, the algorithm will not provide clarity. It won't pause to ask why. It will take your ambiguity and run with it—executing indecision with chilling efficiency.

So, this chapter is something of a pivot point. It is where theory and intention must converge. A place to take the fragments of understanding from earlier discussions—about risk, complexity, emotion, and automation—and begin shaping them into something durable. Not a ready-made doctrine. Certainly not a checklist. But a philosophy that lives and breathes: a structure of thought built from conviction, sustained by chosen tools, refined through habit. Something supple enough to adapt with the market, yet steady enough to anchor you when sentiment swells or confidence falters. A frame of mind, if you like, that can evolve alongside both technology and self—without losing sight of either.

### From Tactics to Strategy: Why Most Investors Stay Shallow

Investment culture often rewards cleverness over clarity. It lionises those who pick the right moment, arbitrage a temporary inefficiency, or game a system faster than others. This tactical obsession is not neutral—it is structural. It distracts from the deeper work of articulating what kind of investor you are, what you're willing to risk, and what success means on your terms.

The result is fragmentation: smart people with sophisticated dashboards but no coherent worldview. An AI tool here, a momentum trade there, an ESG screen bolted onto a portfolio that contradicts it in practice. The antidote is not more data, more dashboards, or more news feeds. It's *less scattered action and more strategic thought.*

This is the essence of the philosophy of strategy: treating every tactic as subordinate to a coherent long-term orientation. What guides your decisions when markets are calm is what stabilises them when markets convulse. A real philosophy is not about rigidity. It's about consistency *through adaptability*.

## Choosing an AI Toolkit That Reflects *You*

The rise of AI in investing is both a revolution and a trap. A revolution, because it allows for hyper-personalisation, deep pattern detection, and real-time adaptability in ways that were previously unimaginable. A trap, because it seduces with abstraction and defers too easily to complexity.

Your task is not to become a quant. It is to become *selectively literate* in the tools that serve your actual goals. Choosing an AI toolkit is not a procurement decision; it's a philosophical alignment exercise. Which tools reflect how you think about risk, return, uncertainty, and ethics? Which platforms nudge you towards understanding—and which numb you with simulation?

There is no universal recommendation here because there is no universal investor. Some may need anomaly detectors tuned to volatility clusters. Others may benefit more from AI-assisted ESG scoring algorithms that align with their moral compass. The key insight is this: *your technology choices are value choices*. Treat them as such.

## Reflection as Practice, Not Post-Mortem

The intelligent use of AI is not just about inputs—it is about *reflection loops*. And yet, almost no investor makes structured reflection part of their strategy. They review trades, not thoughts. They monitor results, not reasoning. They adjust risk, not philosophy.

One of the most overlooked disciplines in advanced investing is *investment journaling*. Not for performance metrics, but for *metacognitive clarity*. Why did I make that decision? What data did I ignore? What emotion was I pretending not to feel? Over time, these reflections form a longitudinal map of your thinking. They become a mirror—revealing patterns, blind spots, and breakthroughs that no algorithm can deliver.

The best investors treat their strategy as a hypothesis. It must be tested, not worshipped. This chapter encourages the practice of regular philosophical audits: scheduled periods of disciplined reflection where you review not just what your investments are doing, but *what they are saying about you.*

## Integrating Purpose Without Diluting Performance

There is a modern anxiety that purpose and performance are mutually exclusive. That if you invest with moral clarity, you must forgo returns. That values erode edge. But this is a false binary. The deeper truth is this: *values are not a constraint on performance—they are a constraint on regret.*

In an AI-enhanced world, it is easy to optimise everything but meaning. But if your investment philosophy doesn't integrate purpose, then no matter how efficient it is, it will always be hollow. Purpose isn't a layer you add later. It's the logic that determines how you define "enough," where you draw ethical lines, and why you continue to participate in the system at all.

Living with machines means more than delegating tasks. It means maintaining human discernment at the centre of your financial identity. Your AI-enhanced investment philosophy must reflect not just what you can do, but what *should* be done—by you, for reasons that make sense in your own ethical grammar.

## The End Is a Beginning

This chapter does not present a finished product. It presents a methodology: to approach your investment life with the seriousness of a moral project, the adaptability of a systems thinker, and the humility of someone aware that no tool, no model, and no machine will ever eliminate the need for judgement.

AI will not replace you as an investor. But it may reveal how replaceable your thinking has become—unless you do the work of *building your philosophy before you automate your action.*

What follows is not doctrine. It is design space. Here you will find frameworks, prompts, and disciplines—not to tell you what to believe, but to help you architect a belief system robust enough to evolve. The future of investing does not belong to the fastest. It belongs to those who can move fast *without losing themselves.*

Let's build that investor now.

## The Philosophy of Strategy

*Encouraging readers to move from scattered tactics to a cohesive long-term approach guided by principles*

Strategy, in the context of investing, is one of the most overused and least understood concepts. It is often mistaken for planning, confused with forecasting, or reduced to an amalgamation of tactics dressed in jargon. But true strategy—philosophical, durable, and self-refining—is not about anticipating the future. It is about preparing for it with coherence.

The strategic investor is not the one with the most sophisticated algorithm, nor the one who reacts fastest to market volatility. It is the one who understands *why* they act the way they do, *what* principles govern those actions, and *how* those principles endure amid noise, complexity, and technological acceleration. In the age of AI, where the informational edge is eroding and speed is commodified, *a well-reasoned strategy may be the last sustainable advantage.*

This article challenges the reader to move beyond episodic decisions, market timing attempts, or the latest tool acquisition. It calls for something more fundamental: a reorientation toward long-term philosophical clarity, a scaffolding for investment behaviour that remains intelligible even when the world does not.

## Strategy Is Not a Plan—It Is a Pattern of Thinking

A plan is a sequence of steps directed at a known outcome. Strategy, by contrast, deals with environments of uncertainty, incomplete information, and adversarial dynamics. Planning assumes control; strategy *acknowledges complexity*. In investing, where randomness and reflexivity dominate, plans fail often. Strategy, when anchored in sound philosophy, *survives*.

The key difference is epistemological. Plans rest on prediction. Strategies rest on interpretation. A good strategy adapts because it is structured around questions of principle: *What is worth pursuing? What is worth avoiding? What risks are tolerable, and for whom?*

The philosopher-statesman Charles de Gaulle once wrote, "*Nothing great will ever be achieved without great men, and men are great only if they are determined to be so.*" Substitute "men" with "strategies", and the point remains: greatness in investing is rarely an accident. It is usually a result of disciplined commitment to something deeper than quarterly returns.

## The Problem with Tactics: Data-Rich, Meaning-Poor

Much of modern investing is tactical by default. Investors, retail and institutional alike, often operate with fragmented objectives: reduce volatility, seek alpha, track ESG scores, hedge currency exposure, and so on. They adopt platforms, follow signals, and interpret models—but seldom step back to ask *why* they are doing what they are doing, or *how* each tactic serves a unified philosophy.

This tactical fragmentation is compounded by the tools themselves. AI-enabled platforms offer convenience, not coherence. They allow for precision without perspective. And they do not care whether the investor deploying them understands their implications.

Take for example an investor who uses a sentiment analysis model to time entry into crypto markets, while simultaneously holding long-term positions in carbon-neutral ETFs to express a values-based worldview. The contradiction is not just aesthetic—it reflects a deeper incoherence. *Without a philosophical filter, tactics become contradictory by default.*

### The Philosophical Turn: Coherence Before Calculation

A genuine investment philosophy is not about maximising return. It is about *optimising alignment* between one's goals, values, risk tolerance, time horizon, and beliefs about how markets behave. It resists the temptation to chase every signal and instead prioritises *internal coherence.*

Philosophy in this context means sustained reflection on the following:

*What do I believe about the nature of markets?* Are they efficient, chaotic, reflexive, or gamified?

*What does "wealth" mean to me?* Is it security, status, legacy, or freedom?

*What am I willing to lose?* Not just financially, but psychologically or ethically?

*What role should technology play in my decisions?* Should it guide, confirm, or simply inform?

These questions do not resolve into formulas. But they do yield clarity. And from that clarity, coherent strategy emerges.

### A Historical Interlude: Why Strategy Beats Genius

Consider Benjamin Graham and Warren Buffett—perhaps the two most referenced names in investment literature. Both are widely admired not because they predicted more accurately than others, but because they developed and adhered to *systems of thought.* Graham's value-investing framework was grounded in psychological realism: markets are emotional, so investors must be rational. Buffett's philosophy, as it evolved, added a filter for quality, temperament, and trust in business leadership.

Neither operated by reacting to economic news or buying into short-term themes. They operated on the basis of articulated, consistent principles. That is what made their success replicable in logic, if not in results.

Contrast this with countless hedge fund managers who generate one or two years of astronomical returns and then vanish—victims of overfitting, overconfidence, or market regime shifts. Their downfall is rarely a lack of intelligence. It is often *the absence of a philosophy that could survive structural change.*

**Strategic Literacy in an AI World**

Artificial intelligence has made it possible to detect micro-patterns in real-time, forecast short-term flows, and backtest strategies across thousands of hypothetical regimes. But AI cannot tell you which *outcomes matter to you.* Nor can it define what *you* are solving for.

Strategic literacy in the age of AI requires two simultaneous disciplines:

1. *Technological discernment*: Knowing which tools align with your philosophical commitments. For example, using predictive analytics to better manage downside risk is coherent for someone whose philosophy emphasises capital preservation. But using the same tool to trade momentum in markets one barely understands may reflect a philosophical vacuum.

2. *Narrative clarity*: Being able to explain—clearly and concisely—why your portfolio looks the way it does. Not just in terms of exposure or diversification, but in terms of *purpose.* Can you articulate why you own what you own in the context of a worldview?

The danger of AI is not that it misleads. It is that it *displaces reflection with simulation.* It makes decisions *feel* intelligent, even when they are philosophically hollow.

### How to Begin: Principles as the Foundation of Action

A strategy guided by philosophy begins with principle. Principles are not rules; they are heuristics rooted in belief. For instance:

*I believe markets are inefficient in the short term, but tend toward rationality over longer horizons.*

*I prefer transparent business models over opaque ones, even if it means sacrificing some return.*

*I will not invest in companies whose core operations I do not understand.*

*I accept underperformance during certain cycles as a cost of philosophical integrity.*

From such principles, strategic architecture unfolds naturally. Asset allocation becomes a function of belief, not trend. Risk tolerance is defined by values, not volatility metrics. Tools are chosen to serve strategy—not the other way around.

### The Role of Review: Strategy as a Living Document

Even the best philosophies evolve. The strategic investor knows that beliefs are not dogmas, but hypotheses under continuous review. Regular philosophical audits—not just financial reviews—are essential. Ask yourself:

Have my core beliefs changed based on new evidence?

Are there inconsistencies in my portfolio that reflect a drift from my stated principles?

Am I still solving for the outcomes I claim to care about?

These questions ensure that strategy remains *dynamic without becoming reactive.* They also prevent the slow erosion of coherence that often accompanies growth, complexity, and external pressure.

### Final Thoughts: You Cannot Outsource Thinking

In a world awash with smart tools, real intelligence lies in synthesis. The ability to integrate tools, tactics, data, and beliefs into a coherent whole is not a feature of software—it is a feature of strategy.

The philosopher of strategy is not someone who rejects technology or data. It is someone who *uses them consciously*, in service of something more enduring than this quarter's return.

You cannot outsource your investment thinking. But you can elevate it—by grounding it in a philosophy worth returning to, especially when the market invites panic and the machine offers a shortcut.

Start there. Stay there. And build forward.

## Curating Your AI Toolkit: Choosing Tools, Platforms, and Advisors That Truly Align

Some tools are designed to dazzle; others to guide. In the world of AI-driven investing, the line between the two is often blurred—intentionally so. As machine intelligence becomes embedded in everything from robo-advisors to sentiment-scraping algorithms, the question isn't whether you should use AI. The question is *which AI you should trust, and why*.

This subchapter isn't a survey of trending platforms or a roundup of tech specs. It is a strategic lens—an attempt to help you build a *principled*, high-agency relationship with the AI tools shaping your financial decisions. Because while the digital age has made many things easier, it has also made the intelligent investor's task harder: *How do you maintain clarity of purpose when your tools are optimised for speed, scale, and seduction—not alignment?*

Let us begin, not with what to choose, but how to choose.

### The Philosophy of Alignment: Tools as Extensions of Values

Before selecting any AI platform, investors must first confront a philosophical baseline: *tools are never neutral.* Every algorithm encodes a set of assumptions. Every platform operationalises a worldview. Whether it's a risk-tolerance quiz, a trading bot, or a portfolio optimiser, the AI you use *is not just a calculator*—it's a strategist acting on your behalf, often invisibly. If you don't interrogate its logic, you're not augmenting your judgement—you're outsourcing it.

Ask not just "What does this tool do?" but:

*What theory of risk is this tool assuming?*

*How does it define success—alpha, stability, ESG impact, resilience?*

*Does it reinforce my worst impulses or sharpen my best discipline?*

These are not cosmetic questions. They determine whether your AI infrastructure functions as a compass—or as a casino.

### Contextual Intelligence: Matching Tools to Strategic Depth

There is a dangerous seduction in delegating complexity. AI tools promise real-time updates, predictive analytics, behavioural nudges, and portfolio rebalancing with a click. But sophistication in output is meaningless without sophistication in context.

A day trader in volatile crypto markets will require a fundamentally different toolkit than a long-horizon ESG-oriented institutional allocator. Yet both may find themselves tempted by the same dashboards, alerts, and "insights."

A discerning investor evaluates tools based on *fit for purpose.* Here are a few key distinctions that help establish that fit:

**Time Horizon**: Is your strategy short-term tactical or long-term thematic? High-frequency signals may introduce unnecessary noise for patient capital.

**Risk Philosophy**: Are you volatility-tolerant or drawdown-averse? Some AI engines optimise for Sharpe ratios, others for downside protection.

**Impact Orientation**: If ESG matters to you, ask how (not whether) the tool integrates it. Does it quantify governance as a score, or is it scraping board minutes for meaningful red flags?

**Behavioural Alignment**: Does the tool help you regulate fear and greed—or does it amplify dopamine loops under the guise of "gamification"?

These aren't technical specs; they're *philosophical boundaries.* Tools must not just be impressive—they must be coherent with your strategy's inner architecture.

**Transparency and Explainability: No Black Boxes Without Accountability**

The deeper your dependence on AI, the higher the cost of opacity. Tools that can't explain their logic—or worse, don't allow you to audit their decision pathways—are not partners in intelligence. They're automated authorities.

Explainability, a principle often discussed in AI ethics, is critical in finance. If an algorithm adjusts your exposure to China because it detects "increased sentiment volatility" based on NLP models trained on Weibo data, you must know:

What data sources were used?

What biases were embedded in the model's training?

Is the signal repeatable, or merely retrospective noise?

Sophisticated investors demand not just performance but *interpretability.* A tool that cannot justify its recommendations in human language should be treated not as a co-pilot, but as a liability.

### The Human Layer: Beyond Tools, Toward Relationships

Curating your AI stack is not just about choosing software—it's about choosing which *human+machine combinations* you are willing to trust. Whether through a wealth manager using proprietary models, or a firm offering AI-augmented financial planning, you're not choosing code; you're choosing *judgement ecosystems.*

The most valuable platforms will not just offer tools—they will facilitate *dialogue*, reflection, and feedback loops. They will treat you not as a user, but as a *thinking partner.* The best advisors—digital or flesh-and-blood—will:

Help you frame trade-offs, not just optimise returns

Invite strategic questioning, not just compliance with output

Encourage periodic audits of your toolset against evolving goals

It is in these relational structures—not in feature sets or performance charts—that the real durability of an AI-enhanced strategy is found.

### Curate, Don't Accumulate: The Discipline of Subtraction

The temptation to add just one more AI tool—to monitor sentiment, backtest momentum, flag anomalies—is endless. But strategic clarity is not a function of dashboard density. It is the result of *disciplined subtraction.* Choose fewer tools, but know them deeply. Understand not just how they operate, but *how they shape your thinking.*

The investor of the future will not be the one with the most APIs, but the one with the most *discernment* about which AI inputs matter, and which are merely noise dressed as novelty.

### Periodic Review: Your Toolkit Needs a Philosophy of Renewal

Like portfolios, toolkits drift. Assumptions calcify. Tools lose relevance as strategies evolve. That's why your AI infrastructure should be reviewed not just for performance, but for *philosophical integrity.*

Ask yourself quarterly:

Have my goals shifted in ways this tool no longer serves?

Has this tool started to shape my behaviour in ways that reduce my agency?

Is there a better way to generate this insight—either through human conversation or better data logic?

Tools should serve strategy, not the reverse.

### A Closing Challenge: Build Your Stack Like a Thinker, Not a Trend-Follower

The AI revolution in investing is not a threat to human judgement. It is a mirror that reveals its contours. Used well, AI can sharpen conviction, broaden foresight, and discipline emotion. Used poorly, it can reduce investors to *reactive tacticians*, forever chasing the next model, metric, or market signal.

Your toolkit is your signal to yourself. It reveals whether you are building your investing life on noise, or on clarity. Choose tools not for what they promise—but for what they *make possible* when aligned with wisdom.

Because in the end, the only toolkit worth curating is the one that helps you remain more fully human in the presence of the machine.

## The Role of Reflection and Revision: Why Investment Journaling and Philosophical Audits Matter More Than Ever

Most investors spend their time looking outward—at markets, data feeds, macro indicators, or portfolio dashboards. Very few look inward. Fewer still do so systematically. And yet, in a world increasingly saturated with artificial intelligence, machine-optimised decision-making, and digital over-stimulation, *the most underutilised competitive edge is not faster execution—it's deeper reflection.*

What if the most meaningful investment alpha came not from a new model, platform, or thesis, but from a more deliberate relationship with your own thinking?

This is the premise of reflective investing: a deliberate practice of *watching your mind work*, not merely watching your assets move. The tools? Simple. An honest journal. A structured process. A periodic philosophical audit. The result? *Clarity, continuity, and coherence*—qualities that no algorithm can deliver on your behalf.

Let's take this seriously, because it deserves to be taken seriously.

**Why Reflection Is a Strategic Necessity, Not a Sentimental Luxury**

There is a widespread misconception—especially in high-performance domains—that reflection is introspective fluff. Tactical irrelevance. "Nice to have" but not essential. In finance, where rationality is fetishised and speed is glorified, reflection is often treated like ballast.

But this view is short-sighted. Markets do not reward speed alone. They reward *resilience, coherence, and the capacity to adapt thoughtfully under uncertainty*. These are not algorithmic virtues; they are *cognitive virtues*. And they can only be cultivated through deliberate feedback with yourself.

More specifically:

Reflection *makes your decisions legible*. It allows you to track not only what you did, but why you did it.

It *surfaces cognitive distortions* before they calcify into habits.

It *clarifies your risk philosophy* as it evolves—not merely in theory but in practice.

It enables *meta-cognition*—thinking about how you think—so your judgement becomes more self-aware, not just more informed.

In a noisy world, reflection is not soft. It is signal.

**Investment Journaling: A Practice of Cognitive Traceability**

Think of an investment journal as a personal ledger—not of trades, but of thoughts. It's not a diary. It's a structured record of what you believed, what you expected, what you feared, and what you felt *at the time of action.*

Done properly, journaling creates cognitive traceability. It allows you to go back and see: "What was my logic?" Not the logic you wish you had. The logic you actually used.

This is crucial, because memory is an unreliable narrator. Without records, we misremember our predictions as more accurate, our reasoning as more coherent, and our past selves as more disciplined than they were. *Journaling breaks that illusion.*

Here's what a practical investment entry might include:

**Date** and context

**Decision made** (buy/sell/hold/change allocation)

**Hypothesis** (Why do I believe this is the right move?)

**Anticipated risks** (What am I afraid of? What could go wrong?)

**Time horizon** (When will I revisit this? What would make me change my mind?)

**Emotional state** (How do I feel—anxious, confident, reactive, reflective?)

You can write it in shorthand. You can keep it on paper, in Notion, or embedded in your investment platform. What matters is not format. *What matters is fidelity*—an honest capture of your real-time thinking.

### Periodic Review: The Audit of Intention vs. Action

But journaling alone is not enough. Reflection becomes powerful when it is *iterative.* That is: when you review what you wrote, not just record it.

Set aside time—quarterly or annually—for a structured audit. Not just of your portfolio's performance, but of your *thinking performance.*

Ask:

How often did my decisions align with my long-term principles?

When did I let emotions override strategy?

Which beliefs did I revise—and why?

What patterns of impatience, overconfidence, or neglect do I notice?

Are my tools still aligned with my intentions—or have I adapted my philosophy to fit my tools?

These are not questions for entertainment. They are questions for *alignment*—between principle and practice, between the investor you intend to be and the one you are becoming.

Think of this as a *philosophical P&L.* Not profit and loss in capital, but in *conviction, clarity, and consistency.*

### Why Even the Most Rational Strategies Drift Without Reflection

There is a law of entropy in investing—not just in portfolios, but in people. Without conscious recalibration, we drift.

Our risk tolerance decays under the pressure of short-term volatility. Our time horizon contracts in response to media noise. Our conviction weakens with each market shock. And slowly, almost imperceptibly, *our strategy becomes reactive.*

Reflection interrupts that drift. It provides a mirror. It re-centres us in *first principles*.

This is particularly urgent in the AI age, where the pace of feedback is exponential—but the quality of introspection is lagging. As machine-generated signals increase, the temptation to abandon personal strategy in favour of crowdsourced conviction becomes stronger. Reflection is the only antidote.

Without it, the investor is not a strategist—but a spectator.

**Philosophical Audits: From Tactical Adjustments to Strategic Coherence**

Journaling helps you track micro-decisions. But philosophical audits help you interrogate macro-architecture. They ask: *Does the framework still serve the vision?*

Every six or twelve months, conduct a deeper audit. This is not a portfolio review. It's a *values review*. You're not assessing beta exposure—you're evaluating alignment.

Consider framing it with questions like:

What is my actual definition of "risk" today—not the textbook one?

Is my strategy shaped more by fear avoidance or value pursuit?

Have I mistaken complexity for sophistication?

Am I being *led by my tools*, or am I *leading through my tools*?

What has changed in my worldview since the last audit—and how should my strategy evolve accordingly?

This practice doesn't require a guru. It requires a chair, an hour, and a refusal to pretend that your philosophy is finished.

### Reflection Is Not About Perfection—It's About Pattern Recognition

A final caution: reflection is not a spiritual quest for infallibility. You will still make bad calls. You will still overreact, underprepare, or misread a signal. That is not failure. That is feedback.

The goal of journaling and auditing is *pattern awareness*. To build a corpus of insight over time. To notice where your blind spots recur. To trace the difference between noise and signal in your own mental process. To distinguish one-time mistakes from systemic misalignments.

Because what we need, now more than ever, is not more hacks—but more *depth*.

### Closing Reflection: Build the Meta-Discipline

In a world where AI can already write memos, backtest trades, optimise allocations, and generate synthetic market commentary, the human edge lies not in out-processing machines—but in *out-reflecting them*.

Investment journaling and philosophical audits are not add-ons. They are *meta-disciplines*—practices that govern the quality of every other decision. They don't just make you a better investor. They make you a more deliberate thinker. And that is a capability no platform, no model, and no algorithm can automate.

Your capital strategy will only ever be as strong as your *reflective capacity*. Sharpen it. Codify it. Honour it with time. Because the investor who thinks about how they think is already operating at a level most never reach.

## Living with Machines, Investing with Meaning

There's a seduction in modern investing that whispers quietly but insistently: *Optimise more, feel less*. As artificial intelligence reshapes every facet of the investment process—from signal extraction to asset allocation to behavioural nudges—the temptation is to yield fully to the machine. To trust the backtest, the model, the algorithmic thesis. And, in doing so, to slowly erode the human foundation beneath it all.

But here's the essential question: *What does it mean to invest well when machines do so much of the "thinking"?*

This subchapter is about regaining ownership. Not of the data, not of the code, but of the *meaning*. It is a reminder that the purpose of investing was never merely to win. It was, and must remain, to align capital with conviction—to allocate not just for returns, but for responsibility, resilience, and relevance.

To live with machines yet invest with meaning is not to reject automation. It is to resist *abdication.*

**From Assistance to Authority: The Evolving Role of AI in Investment Strategy**

AI no longer sits quietly in the background. It doesn't just generate insights; it increasingly proposes actions. Portfolio rebalancing tools, robo-advisory platforms, machine-learning models tuned to factor rotations—all are designed to *reduce friction* and *increase confidence.* But confidence in what?

Too often, in streamlining decisions, these systems also obscure the assumptions behind them. Investors are presented with a clean dashboard but a black-box rationale. What disappears is the *why*—the interpretive layer where values, priorities, and trade-offs reside.

This is not a Luddite alarm. AI *can* be transformative. It can augment judgement, stress-test beliefs, and surface correlations the human eye would never spot. But tools are only as principled as their user. Without human discernment, data becomes noise. Without purpose, optimisation becomes drift.

A disciplined investor must reclaim authorship. Not just of inputs and outputs, but of *interpretation.*

## The Central Tension: Precision vs. Perspective

The core utility of AI is precision. But the core requirement of meaningful investing is *perspective.* And these two are not always in harmony.

A neural network might forecast the next 30 days of price action with uncanny accuracy, yet say nothing of whether that asset contributes to your vision of financial integrity. A language model might synthesise 10,000 earnings calls, but remain silent on whether those companies reflect your ethical boundary lines. Precision solves for tactics. Perspective solves for *trajectory.*

And in moments of uncertainty—when volatility surges or assumptions break—perspective is what remains. Machines may reprice risk. Only humans *reframe meaning.*

This doesn't mean rejecting technological advantage. It means rooting it in *a personal investment philosophy* robust enough to absorb the data without being distorted by it.

## Reframing Performance: Beyond the Quarterly Benchmark

Part of investing with meaning is expanding the definition of performance. Traditional benchmarks measure returns, Sharpe ratios, alpha generation. All valid. But they are incomplete.

Ask:

Did this portfolio reflect my values under pressure, or did it react to noise?

Did I feel in control of my process, or outsourced to a tool I barely understand?

Have I built a system that allows me to sleep well—or merely one that "beats the market"?

These are not sentimental questions. They are strategic ones. *Because misalignment costs more than underperformance—it corrodes trust in your own system.*

An investment strategy that lacks coherence with personal values becomes fragile. When the next drawdown hits, there's no conviction to hold the line. When the next "disruption" trend emerges, there's no filter to judge its relevance. Meaning is not a luxury add-on. It is the mental infrastructure that anchors long-term thinking.

## The Human Advantage: Ethical Filters and Existential Priorities

Let's name what AI cannot do. It cannot assess whether funding a palm oil conglomerate violates your environmental standards. It cannot determine whether a 7% yield justifies investing in a regime that suppresses basic freedoms. It cannot tell you if aligning with speculative crypto projects that monetise attention feels like contribution—or exploitation.

These are questions of *ethics, impact, and purpose.* And they are not edge cases. They are central to any investment practice that claims to be thoughtful.

AI can tell you what is *likely.* Only you can decide what is *right.*

The future of investment practice, therefore, is not a split between human vs. machine. It is a synthesis in which *machines manage complexity, while humans retain context.*

## Building a Philosophy That Withstands the Algorithmic Temptation

How, then, does one construct a system of investing that integrates AI without being overtaken by it? Start not with tools, but with questions.

What do I believe investing is *for*? Accumulation? Freedom? Stewardship?

Which values must *never* be compromised, no matter the model output?

What kind of trade-offs am I willing to make—and where is the line?

When models fail (as all eventually do), what principle will guide me through the ambiguity?

These questions are not academic. They should live in your strategy documents, your investment journals, your decision reviews. They are your compass when systems become opaque.

No amount of predictive power can replace *philosophical clarity*.

**Case in Point: When the Algorithm Is Technically Right—But Strategically Wrong**

Imagine this: your AI platform detects a high-probability, short-term arbitrage opportunity in sovereign bonds issued by a politically unstable regime. The risk-adjusted return is exceptional. The trade is clean, fast, and profitable.

But does it align with your ethics?

Does it match your stated risk tolerance?

Does it advance your goals, or merely exploit a dislocation?

This is where *investing with meaning* departs from simply investing with data. Because your strategy is not just a sequence of trades—it is a narrative of belief, acted out in capital.

And that narrative is what differentiates you from the machine.

**Toward a More Human-Centred Investment Practice**

To live with machines and invest with meaning is to cultivate *dual fluency*—one in technical analysis, one in self-awareness. It is to combine predictive modelling with philosophical inquiry. It is to use the best of modern tools while refusing to surrender moral agency.

This is not easy. But nothing truly worthwhile in investing ever is.

It requires slowing down in places the market wants you to speed up.

It means interrogating "efficiency" as a goal in itself.

It asks you to treat *wisdom* as a valid metric—not just information, not just optimisation.

**The Final Word: Technology as Servant, Never Master**

AI will continue to evolve. It will continue to accelerate, surprise, and outperform. It will make entire categories of analysis obsolete. But it will not—and should not—replace the need for human discernment.

Your role, as an investor living with machines, is to define what matters most *before* the signal floods in. To set the guardrails *before* the volatility hits. To keep purpose front and centre, even as the tools become more autonomous.

Because *meaning is not emergent.* It is designed.

And the investor who designs their system with clarity of values, with ethical backbone, with intentional coherence—will not just survive the age of machines. They will lead it.

# Chapter 10
# The Investor of the Future

What do we truly mean when we call someone a great investor?

Not so long ago, the answer would have sounded familiar: rigorous analysis, the nerve to defy consensus, and that near-mystical ability to feel the market's pulse just before it changed. That image held firm—until, slowly, it didn't. The digital revolution swept in with little ceremony and rewrote the rules. Data multiplied beyond comprehension. Algorithms grew nimble, then dominant. Advantage shifted from instinct to infrastructure. Insight, once won by observation and gut, became a by-product of speed and scale. Analysis didn't disappear—it was simply outpaced. But now, as artificial intelligence tightens its grip and financial systems learn to hum with near-autonomous precision, we find ourselves, once again, at a turning point.

Only this time, the evolution isn't what you might expect. The future of investing does not belong to the person who behaves most like a machine. Precision, speed, and cold logic—while valuable—are no longer rare. They're commodities. Replicable. Scalable. Instead, the real edge will come from something subtler, and frankly, more difficult: being more human, not less. It will come from those who can think in complex systems, sense the intangible, and reflect with uncomfortable honesty on their own assumptions.

This chapter doesn't just tweak the definition of mastery in investing—it rebuilds it. It nudges you away from reactive tinkering and fleeting wins, and points towards a more cohesive, layered orientation: one that integrates emotion, philosophy, and long-term coherence. Not as a nice-to-have, but as a differentiator. Because when tools are abundant and access is near-universal, your advantage won't lie in what you can *use*. It will lie in what you *mean*—in how faithfully your decisions echo your convictions.

## Thinking Like an Ecosystem, Not an Operator

To begin with, a shift in cognition is required. For decades, the dominant mental model in investing has been one of compartmentalisation: equities over here, fixed income over there; alpha separate from beta; winners neatly segregated from losers. But that neatness is an illusion. Today's markets don't live in tidy boxes. They pulse through tangled webs of political risk, planetary boundaries, technological feedback loops, and cascading social shifts. Influence is distributed. Outcomes resist prediction. Impact reverberates in strange, non-linear ways.

This world calls for a different kind of investor. The best among them won't just interpret numbers—they'll interpret systems. They'll be fluent in interconnection, aware of second- and third-order consequences, able to trace how a policy tweak in Brussels ripples through energy markets in Asia and reshapes agricultural futures in Africa. They'll read not only balance sheets, but the context that shapes them: ecological fragility, cultural momentum, ethical undercurrents.

Picture less the image of a lone trader hunched over six monitors, managing exposure to the basis point. Instead, think of someone more akin to a strategist—part philosopher, part steward—mapping the flow of influence across domains.

Now, this isn't some abstract, contemplative idealism. It's a concrete shift in what survival will require. Linear models, those stalwart tools of simpler times, are already faltering. Climate volatility, AI-driven market distortions, political whiplash, even the virality of misinformation—they've all joined forces to create an environment where old tools crack under stress. To remain functional in this environment, let alone successful, one must adapt. Those who fail to make the cognitive leap won't just fall behind. They'll vanish from the conversation entirely.

## Machines May Be Fast—But They Do Not Learn Like Humans

The second shift is epistemological. In the age of large language models and algorithmic forecasting, many investors are wondering: *How do I stay relevant when machines are faster, more objective, and increasingly autonomous?*

The answer is not to out-compete machines on their terms. It is to double down on what they cannot replicate: *long-term curiosity, narrative intelligence, ethical judgement, and adaptive learning.*

The investor of the future must treat lifelong learning not as a personal development slogan but as a fiduciary obligation. That means building a relationship with uncertainty, not by conquering it, but by remaining open, agile, and responsive.

It also means curating diverse sources of insight: cross-disciplinary reading, critical debate, immersion in unfamiliar perspectives. Not just for intellectual enrichment, but to build *cognitive resilience.* In a machine-dominated environment, the human advantage is not in raw information processing—it is in *reframing, questioning,* and *synthesising.*

## The Underrated Edge: Emotional Intelligence

There is a paradox at the heart of modern investing. The more data we have, the more emotionally fragile we become. The more signals we monitor, the more noise we absorb. The more complex our models, the more we outsource our confidence to their outputs.

And so, the investor of the future must cultivate not just analytical acumen, but emotional depth.

Emotional intelligence is not a soft skill in this context—it is *a survival trait.* It governs how we respond to uncertainty, how we manage stress under drawdowns, how we collaborate in high-stakes environments, and how we remain anchored to long-term goals in a culture of instant feedback.

Crucially, emotional intelligence enables *moral clarity*. It allows us to hold tension between competing priorities: profit vs. impact, speed vs. stewardship, data vs. values. It strengthens our ability to make decisions *that feel right*, not just *that test well.*

A spreadsheet won't help you navigate ethical ambiguity. EQ will.

**Towards a New Manifesto for Investing**

This chapter closes with a provocation: *What is your investment philosophy, and is it fit for the future?*

Not your allocation strategy. Not your preferred asset classes. Your philosophy—the core beliefs and principles that guide what you will and won't do with capital. What you measure. What you're accountable to. What you're willing to walk away from.

The investor of the future needs more than a toolkit. They need a *manifesto.*

Not a rigid doctrine, but a living document that holds space for their values, their vision, and their evolving understanding of risk, return, and responsibility. This manifesto must be revisited, challenged, and re-anchored over time. It must remain dynamic—because the world it navigates will be anything but static.

It is through this lens that we will explore the final components of the future-ready investor:

How to see yourself as *a participant in systems*, not just a user of tools.

How to structure learning, *not just consume information.*

How to treat emotion as *an input*, not a liability.

And how to *invest with intentionality*, not just efficiency.

Each section is a layer in a broader framework that aims not just to improve returns, but to improve *investment as a practice.* Not just to optimise for now, but to future-proof what it means to invest well—in every sense of the word.

## From Individual to Ecosystem Thinker

The modern investor, for all the tools at their disposal—real-time data, algorithmic models, on-demand analytics—often remains intellectually stranded in a framework that is outdated. The paradigm of isolated stock picking, divorced from context and consequence, no longer holds. In a world shaped by interdependency, systemic fragility, and emergent complexity, the future investor must evolve. *Strategy divorced from systems thinking is not only naive—it is hazardous.*

The traditional approach to investing has long been anchored in reductionism. Isolate a security, dissect its financials, compare ratios, execute a trade. This methodology—bred in the age of Warren Buffett's early letters and Benjamin Graham's value logic—made sense when markets were less globalised, less entangled, and less volatile. But today, single-variable thinking is insufficient. An investor may identify an undervalued company, but if that company's supply chain threads through politically unstable regions, if its ESG profile triggers algorithmic disinvestment by major funds, or if its core product becomes obsolete due to an AI-induced shift in demand—the thesis unravels.

*Systems thinking* is not a rejection of traditional analysis, but its expansion. It requires the investor to ask different questions: What is the feedback loop between this company and its environment? How will this asset behave under non-linear stress? What dependencies, both visible and latent, shape its future viability? These are not academic indulgences—they are strategic imperatives.

### The Fallacy of Fragmented Thinking

The most dangerous illusion in finance is the belief that parts can be understood in isolation. Financial education has long encouraged segmentation: equities here, commodities there, fixed income in another silo. Even risk is categorised separately—credit risk, market risk, operational risk—as if these operate independently. Yet, the 2008 global financial crisis exposed the absurdity of such compartmentalisation. A failure in subprime mortgages cascaded through derivatives markets, crippled liquidity, and required geopolitical coordination to resolve. What began as a sector-specific problem revealed itself as an ecosystemic failure.

This pattern has only intensified. Climate change affects agricultural yields, which in turn influence commodity prices, insurance models, and sovereign risk. Social unrest triggered by inequality or misinformation ripples into market sentiment, consumption patterns, and regulatory crackdowns. *Everything is connected, and often in ways we fail to model adequately.*

## From Portfolio Construction to Ecological Awareness

Ecosystem thinking in investing means shifting from allocation to integration. A portfolio is no longer merely a bundle of assets—it is a *narrative* of how one believes the world works. If you believe in the resilience of decentralised systems, your portfolio will tilt toward blockchain infrastructure. If you believe in geopolitical fragmentation, you will overweight critical minerals and national defence. If you see water scarcity as a defining constraint, you will include utilities and desalination tech. This is no longer abstract positioning; it is *philosophy translated into allocation.*

Moreover, systems thinking encourages temporal layering. Investors often debate time horizons, yet rarely appreciate how different timeframes carry distinct assumptions about system stability. A five-year investment in urban real estate assumes political continuity, infrastructure maintenance, and demographic predictability. A 20-year bet on carbon capture assumes both technological viability and policy enforcement. Systems thinking demands that we *explicitly model the fragility of those assumptions*, not merely project returns.

## Feedback Loops, Tipping Points, and Hidden Interactions

One of the most difficult challenges in systems-based investing is navigating feedback loops—processes where cause and effect amplify or dampen each other. AI-driven trading is a prime example. Predictive models influence trades, which in turn shift markets, which then feed back into the model's data. This creates reflexivity: the system acts on its own predictions. As George Soros once noted, *"Market participants are not merely observers but also actors."*

A seemingly rational decision—like reallocating assets away from fossil fuels—can trigger unintended systemic reactions: energy price volatility, stranded assets, and political resistance. Recognising these loops is not about paralysis, but preparation. *Investors who cannot perceive second- and third-order effects are investors walking blindfolded into complexity.*

Tipping points are another feature of ecosystems: moments when gradual change becomes sudden transformation. Think of the collapse of Lehman Brothers, or the depegging of the Swiss franc. These are not outliers; they are reminders that systems behave differently near critical thresholds. Risk metrics that assume normal distributions fail catastrophically in such environments. Thus, investors must learn to think like ecologists—aware of thresholds, warning signs, and cascading failure.

## Why This Shift is Philosophical, Not Merely Technical

This is not simply a matter of using better software or integrating ESG dashboards. It is a shift in *epistemology*—how we understand knowledge itself. Traditional finance encourages prediction; systems thinking emphasises *adaptation.* Classical models seek precision; systems frameworks prioritise *resilience.* In a world where the future is not just unknown but *unknowable*, this distinction matters.

The individualistic ethos of prior investing philosophies—master the data, outsmart the market, dominate the trade—must yield to a more relational logic. Ecosystem thinkers understand that *context is king*, that ethics shape markets, and that intelligence without humility leads to ruin.

### Case Study: COVID-19 and Investment Myopia

Consider the early days of the COVID-19 pandemic. Investors who viewed the virus as a healthcare issue were late. Those who recognised its systemic potential—supply chains, consumer behaviour, policy response—repositioned early. The best-performing funds of 2020 were not merely agile; they were *structurally perceptive*. They grasped that the pandemic was not a discrete event but an *ecosystemic stress test*.

The lesson? It's not about prediction; it's about perception. Seeing the whole picture faster than others is the new alpha.

### Practical Implications for Today's Investor

To move from individual to ecosystem thinker requires more than a shift in mindset; it demands tools and discipline:

**Mental models** must broaden beyond CAPM and Sharpe ratios to include complexity theory, scenario mapping, and systems archetypes.

**Research must diversify**: Not only financial reports, but climate models, geopolitical briefings, technological roadmaps.

**Diversity in networks** becomes essential. Systems are best understood through multidisciplinary lenses—collaborate with environmental scientists, sociologists, policy experts.

**Humility must be engineered** into decision-making. This means pre-mortems, red-teaming, and critical audits of one's own biases.

None of these steps can guarantee outperformance in the short term. But they *do* maximise adaptability—a currency more precious than precision in a volatile world.

### The Investor as Citizen

Finally, ecosystem thinking carries a moral dimension. Investment choices ripple outward. Capital shapes behaviours, institutions, and outcomes. Where you allocate funds affects labour conditions, climate trajectories, and social cohesion. To deny this is not objectivity; it is negligence. As systems become more visible, so too does responsibility. *Tomorrow's investor must be fluent in complexity—and accountable to consequence.*

## Lifelong Learning in a Machine World

There is no standing still in a landscape where software rewrites itself, capital moves at sub-second speeds, and yesterday's competitive edge becomes tomorrow's historical footnote. The modern financial professional—whether investor, analyst, policymaker, or entrepreneur—is no longer contending with periodic updates or occasional disruption. *They are operating inside an accelerating system*, one where knowledge decays rapidly, and static expertise is quietly but decisively punished.

This is not a passing phase or the crest of a temporary wave. The integration of artificial intelligence into financial markets has ushered in an ontological shift. The machine no longer merely assists—it interprets, forecasts, adapts, and in some cases, makes decisions without human supervision. What this means for the thoughtful investor is not that human judgement is obsolete. It means that human judgement, *to remain relevant*, must become more adaptive, more self-reflective, and critically—*more committed to lifelong learning.*

The paradox is striking: we are surrounded by systems that learn continuously, yet many of their creators do not. While we praise agile algorithms, the human tendency is often intellectual ossification—clinging to old frameworks, resisting uncomfortable information, or mistaking early competence for enduring insight. This is more than a cognitive trap; in financial terms, it is a liability.

### Why Static Knowledge is a Risk Factor

Finance has always rewarded pattern recognition. The most celebrated investors—from George Soros to Ray Dalio—excelled not just because of their models, but because they updated those models in real time, guided by new evidence and emergent anomalies. Today, the half-life of a financial insight has shortened dramatically. A novel arbitrage strategy or an edge in sentiment analysis may last weeks, sometimes days, before being subsumed by the broader ecosystem.

The cost of outdated knowledge is no longer marginal—it is systemic. Consider the investor trained in pre-2008 models of credit risk. Their tools may not even *register* the signals that flagged the mortgage crisis. Or the economist schooled in rational expectations theory, blind to behavioural finance breakthroughs that have since redefined our understanding of market irrationality. Even an expert in blockchain from 2016 is ill-equipped to parse today's tokenised ecosystems without a rigorous programme of re-skilling.

In this environment, *being smart is not enough.* One must be *adaptive*—intellectually elastic, epistemologically humble, and strategically restless.

### Reframing Learning as Strategic Infrastructure

The investor of the future must treat learning not as a peripheral hobby but as a *core function of professional survival.* This reframing has practical implications. Just as one allocates time to portfolio review, risk audits, or earnings reports, time must be carved out for structured learning. This is not an aspirational gesture—it is infrastructure.

What does this look like in practice?

**Designated intellectual sprints**: Set aside regular periods—weekly, monthly, quarterly—for structured inquiry into emerging fields, whether that's AI interpretability, decentralised autonomous organisations, or post-carbon economics.

**Reverse mentorship**: Surround yourself with domain fluency outside your generation, geography, or training. Those 20 years younger or working in climate tech or game theory may hold the lens you're missing.

**Learning portfolios**: Document the evolution of your knowledge with the same discipline as you would a financial portfolio. What were your hypotheses? What did you misread? What assumptions did you abandon—and why?

This last point is not academic. The practice of *meta-cognition*—thinking about how you think—is perhaps the most underutilised skill in financial circles. It's what separates the reactive from the resilient.

### Navigating the Noise: Curation as a Critical Skill

The abundance of information is both a gift and a toxin. Today, access is no longer the bottleneck. Discernment is. The intelligent investor must become a ruthless curator. This requires more than subscribing to well-known journals or listening to popular finance podcasts. It demands the cultivation of *filters*—ethical, epistemological, and strategic.

Which voices align with your values? Which analyses are methodologically sound rather than emotionally persuasive? Which thinkers challenge your assumptions rather than confirm them?

This process also extends to tools. The machine-learning boom has produced an ecosystem of dashboards, signal generators, NLP-based scrapers, and trading bots. But too much tooling leads to a fragmentation of focus. The disciplined learner asks: *Which tools sharpen my understanding, and which merely simulate it?*

## The Psychology of Staying Curious

Curiosity, once treated as a personality trait, must now be managed as a discipline. That means confronting psychological inertia head-on. The human brain is wired for cognitive ease—it prefers known routines, familiar conclusions, and mental shortcuts. But these comforts are lethal in a machine world.

Lifelong learning therefore demands a posture of *structured discomfort.* You must be willing to feel cognitively stretched, temporarily incompetent, occasionally overwhelmed. These sensations are not signals of failure; they are evidence that you are operating near your learning frontier.

This is not masochism—it is *growth by design.* Investors should not merely track P&Ls. They should track cognitive expansion.

## Relevance Over Recall

In a machine world, encyclopaedic knowledge loses its edge. The AI can index, recall, and summarise with superhuman efficiency. What the machine cannot replicate—at least not yet—is the human ability to contextualise, synthesise, and judge *relevance.*

This means that the core question for human learners is no longer "Do I know this?" but rather, "*Does this matter now?*" and "*What does this change about what I thought I knew?*"

This shift has consequences for education at every level. The MBA student memorising financial formulas is investing in a skill the machine already exceeds. The lifelong investor who instead learns *how those formulas fail in the real world*—during liquidity crises, under behavioural distortions, amid regulatory shifts—is training for resilience.

## From Consumption to Creation

Perhaps the final frontier in lifelong learning is not information intake, but intellectual output. There is no better test of understanding than the act of *creating*. Write an internal memo. Present a contrarian thesis. Build a model from first principles. Teach a concept to someone outside your domain.

These acts convert passive knowledge into *active insight*. They forge neural pathways the machine cannot replicate because they are *yours*, steeped in your context, values, and experiences.

This is not romanticism. It is *strategic differentiation*. In a future where AI may equalise informational access, the investor who can generate original thought—deep, rigorous, human—retains a lasting edge.

### Conclusion Without Concluding

There is no arrival point in lifelong learning. No final syllabus, no terminal degree, no definable mastery. The modern investor must adopt an *infinite mindset*—one that values adaptability over authority, curiosity over certainty, and resilience over reputation.

In a machine world, you are not in competition with the AI. You are in competition with your former self. And the only question worth asking is: *Are you evolving faster than the system you seek to master?*

## The Return of Emotional Intelligence

*Why EQ, Not IQ or AI, Defines the Investing Advantage*

For decades, intelligence in finance was narrowly defined. One was either clever enough to beat the market, fast enough to spot inefficiencies, or analytical enough to dissect balance sheets before others could. Intelligence meant IQ. Then, in the 2010s and 2020s, a new frontier emerged: machine intelligence. The logic was compelling—if human cognition is fallible and slow, outsource it to the algorithm. If pattern recognition is key, let the neural networks take over. And in many domains, they did.

But something else was happening, almost imperceptibly, amid the bloom of quant-driven investing and AI-augmented strategy. Markets became saturated with intelligence—*machine intelligence*.

Every firm began using similar sentiment tools, alternative data sources, predictive analytics. As the informational edge flattened, *the emotional edge began to rise in value.*

In a world where smart is cheap and speed is ubiquitous, *what remains rare is equanimity.* The capacity to manage one's reactions, regulate impulses, endure ambiguity, and stay anchored when volatility strikes—these are no longer soft skills. They are *strategic assets.* The future investor is not the one with the most data, but the one most resistant to self-sabotage.

### What Emotional Intelligence Really Means in Markets

Popularised by psychologist Daniel Goleman in the 1990s, emotional intelligence—or EQ—comprises five domains: self-awareness, self-regulation, motivation, empathy, and social skills. On the trading floor or in an investment committee, these are not abstract virtues; they are the invisible infrastructure of sound decision-making.

*Self-awareness* allows investors to distinguish conviction from ego.

*Self-regulation* prevents short-term turbulence from distorting long-term strategy.

*Empathy* enhances stakeholder engagement and counterparty trust.

*Motivation* drives persistence in uncertain conditions.

*Social skills* translate analysis into influence—critical in negotiations, client relations, and team leadership.

In practical terms, emotional intelligence means knowing when to override a model. It means spotting when your confirmation bias is masquerading as insight. It means pausing before a sell-off, not because you're oblivious to the data, but because you recognise *your reaction to the data may be the real risk.*

### Case Study: LTCM vs. Soros

Contrast two emblematic moments in financial history. In 1998, Long-Term Capital Management collapsed spectacularly despite its PhDs and Nobel laureates. Their models failed to account for human irrationality, geopolitical surprise, and correlated panic. Their IQ was never in question. Their *emotional rigidity* was.

Now compare this with George Soros during Black Wednesday in 1992. His infamous bet against the pound was not just a macroeconomic insight—it was also an act of *emotional clarity*. While others hesitated, he executed. Not recklessly, but decisively. Soros himself has said his back pain intensifies when his positions are misaligned with the market—a psychosomatic signal he listens to with clinical seriousness.

This isn't mysticism. It is *embodied awareness*—a quality that eludes both spreadsheets and sentiment bots.

### Why EQ Outperforms in a Machine-Saturated Landscape

Today's financial environment is not constrained by a lack of information. It is constrained by *how humans interact with that information*. The emotional turbulence of retail investors on Reddit, the institutional panic during COVID market crashes, the fragility exposed by bank runs fuelled by real-time social media—all point to one truth: the bottleneck is not the model. *It is the human interpreter.*

And this is where AI fails. AI can process nonlinear relationships, forecast weather disruptions in supply chains, parse earnings calls in milliseconds. But it cannot *feel unease*. It cannot detect the rising dread in a portfolio manager's gut or decode the complex intersubjectivity of a high-stakes negotiation. Nor can it override itself in moments of emotional intensity—because it has no emotions to regulate.

The investor with high EQ does not merely respond to markets. They respond *to themselves*, in markets. That recursive skill is what creates long-term durability. Not intelligence. *Resilience.*

### The Neuroscience of Emotional Fortitude

Recent neuroscience supports this argument. Studies on the prefrontal cortex—the part of the brain responsible for rational planning and impulse control—show that emotionally intelligent individuals have stronger neural connectivity between the amygdala (the threat response centre) and the prefrontal cortex. This allows them to feel fear or excitement without being hijacked by it.

In financial terms, this translates to:

Holding your position during a volatility spike, because your thesis is still sound.

Selling a winning stock not because of FOMO, but because the fundamentals no longer justify the price.

Withstanding prolonged drawdowns without internalising the loss as personal failure.

These behaviours are not products of spreadsheet acumen. They are *emotional postures* developed through intentional cultivation.

### Can EQ Be Trained?

Yes, but not in the way financial analysts are usually trained. It requires reflection, discomfort, feedback, and the development of *meta-cognition*—awareness of one's own mental and emotional states. It's what Ray Dalio refers to when he encourages "radical transparency" at Bridgewater Associates. Or what investor Paul Tudor Jones pursues through mindfulness practices and personal journaling.

Training EQ involves:

Daily debriefs on emotional responses to market moves.

Pre- and post-trade reflections to isolate mood-based decisions.

Psychological audits of decision trees under stress.

Peer feedback that surfaces blind spots and behavioural biases.

None of this is taught in traditional finance programmes. But it should be—because it addresses *the real reason many investors underperform their own portfolios.*

### EQ as the Last True Competitive Advantage

There's a strange irony at play. As more investors rely on quant models and AI-enhanced predictions, the landscape becomes crowded with similar signals. Arbitrage disappears faster. Alpha decays. Edge is harder to sustain.

But EQ is hard to copy. It is not programmable. It is not scalable. It cannot be scraped from the web or built into a dashboard. It is the most *non-transferable asset* in modern investing.

This is why some of the world's best-performing funds now recruit not just for math ability but for emotional steadiness. Why family offices and sovereign wealth funds are more interested in *alignment of values* than exotic strategies. And why, in an increasingly automated landscape, *clients still choose human advisors they trust—not algorithms they admire.*

### Rethinking What It Means to Be Smart

The return of emotional intelligence forces us to redefine smartness. Not as raw analytical horsepower. Not as model sophistication. But as the ability to stay lucid under pressure, curious amid uncertainty, and calm when others are chaotic.

Smartness, in the AI age, is emotional fluency under complexity.

### Final Consideration

As we look toward the future of investing, it is tempting to believe that the machine will do the hard work for us. That all we need is the right signal, the right bot, the right dataset. But the hardest work is still human: *knowing when to trust the model, when to ignore it, and when to act despite its indifference.*

That kind of discernment will not come from code. It will come from you.

## A New Manifesto for Investing

*Principles, Values, and Forward-Facing Intelligence in an AI-Augmented Financial World*

Good investing has never merely been about beating the market. It has always been about understanding it—engaging with risk, time, and capital through a lens that reflects not just one's goals but one's values. But the backdrop has shifted. As artificial intelligence reshapes how information is consumed, interpreted, and executed, the enduring challenge is no longer access to data. It is *alignment*—between tools and temperament, strategy and philosophy, optimisation and meaning.

This subchapter is not a summary. It is a stance. A declaration for how to think about investing as a principled, human endeavour in a computational age. Not a list of techniques. A *compass*. Because tactics become obsolete. Values endure.

### 1. Intelligence Is Ubiquitous. Discernment Is Rare.

Artificial intelligence has flattened the landscape of informational advantage. High-frequency traders and retail investors alike now wield predictive tools, sentiment engines, and satellite-derived commodity insights. What used to be proprietary is now productised. Edge is no longer in knowing more. *It is in knowing what matters.*

This is where discernment—intellectual, emotional, ethical—enters. Knowing *which data to trust*, when to step away from noise, and how to detect the difference between signal and story. AI can run regressions. Only humans can decide what should never be optimised in the first place.

**2. Strategy Must Be Principle-Led, Not Performance-Led.**

The most enduring investment strategies are those grounded in internal coherence—not market mimicry. A principle-led investor does not chase what is trending; they anchor in what is consistent with their values, risk profile, and intellectual temperament.

In practice, this might mean holding unpopular positions during market mania. It may mean exiting with dignity rather than doubling down in denial. Principle-led strategy does not imply rigidity; it implies *integrity*—a logical consistency between ends and means, analysis and action.

**3. The Future Belongs to Investors Who Think in Systems.**

Individual securities exist within ecosystems. A stock is not just a company; it is a node in an industrial, geopolitical, technological, and cultural web. Thinking in silos—sectors, styles, asset classes—leads to fragility. *Thinking in systems leads to resilience.*

This means understanding how supply chain shifts affect currency risk. How ESG regulation in Europe influences bond markets in Asia. How climate volatility reshapes insurance and agriculture simultaneously. The investor of the future must be a cross-disciplinary thinker—capable of zooming out without losing relevance.

**4. Artificial Intelligence Is Not a Strategy. It Is a Mirror.**

AI reflects the biases, assumptions, and incentives embedded within its training data. It will maximise whatever it's instructed to maximise—be that short-term returns, volatility reduction, or engagement metrics. The question is not whether to use AI. The question is *what values you are encoding into your tools.*

For example, if your AI-enhanced portfolio builder is trained to prioritise past returns, it may overweight tech and ignore diversity of sectoral risk. If your signals engine pulls from social media trends, it may favour velocity over validity. *Good investors interrogate their tools as much as their thesis.*

### 5. Risk Is Not Volatility. Risk Is What Cannot Be Undone.

Volatility is discomfort. Risk is consequence. The distinction is not semantic—it is strategic. Many investors conflate short-term swings with long-term danger, or mistake calm periods as signals of safety. The 2008 financial crisis and the 2020 pandemic both emerged from mispriced tail risk, not from poor forecasting models.

This manifesto encourages a different framing: *treat risk as irreversibility.* What can permanently impair capital, trust, or optionality? That is your true exposure. Not standard deviation. Not sentiment. But *what you cannot recover from.*

### 6. Emotional Intelligence Is the Last Sustainable Advantage.

In a marketplace saturated with smartness, calmness becomes rare. In a profession overrun with data, *disciplined introspection becomes differentiating.* The investor who can regulate panic, delay gratification, and cultivate self-awareness will outperform models not because they are smarter, but because they are *less fragile.*

This calls for a reintegration of emotional skills into the investor's toolkit. Journaling, structured debriefs, psychological audits, mindfulness practices—these are not wellness perks. They are *performance infrastructure.* The future of alpha may very well depend on the *emotional balance sheet* as much as the financial one.

### 7. Liquidity Is Not the Same as Freedom.

High liquidity is often framed as a benefit: the freedom to exit at will. But excessive optionality can be paralysing. Investors who constantly toggle strategies, shift timelines, and change philosophies in response to market sentiment often underperform those who commit—*not blindly, but coherently.*

True investing freedom comes not from liquidity but from *clarity*. Knowing why you own what you own. Understanding your thresholds. Setting boundaries in advance. Liquidity is only valuable when paired with *philosophical intentionality.*

**8. Be Wary of the Crowd. But Do Not Dismiss It.**

Contrarianism is not inherently insightful. Sometimes the crowd is right. What distinguishes durable investors is not that they avoid the crowd—it's that they *understand the crowd.* What is motivating this movement? What narratives are fueling the trade? Which incentives are invisible but operative?

GameStop, crypto surges, meme stock oscillations—these were not just market anomalies. They were cultural events. The disciplined investor must be *culturally literate*, even when ideologically distant. *You cannot manage risk you do not understand.*

**9. Build for the Long Now.**

Stewart Brand's concept of the "Long Now" encourages timeframes that stretch beyond one's own lifespan. Investors, too, should be thinking beyond fiscal quarters and market cycles. What capital decisions will age well—not just economically, but ethically?

This means aligning investments with intergenerational outcomes. It means evaluating firms not just by profit, but by *purpose coherence.* It means integrating environmental sustainability, social cohesion, and governance integrity—not because it's fashionable, but because *they are the real levers of future resilience.*

**10. Purpose Is the Ultimate Risk Filter.**

Every investor faces a deluge of opportunity. AI will only amplify this: more strategies, more signals, more access. The temptation is constant. But clarity comes not from adding filters—it comes from *knowing your purpose.* A well-defined purpose filters noise better than any algorithm.

Ask: What am I solving for? What am I unwilling to compromise on? What is my definition of enough? The clearer your answers, the sharper your lens for strategy, tool selection, and risk appetite.

### Final Thought: The Ethical Investor Is the Future Investor

As finance becomes more machine-augmented, the human layer becomes more crucial—not less. Values, ethics, discernment, and emotional fluency are no longer philosophical luxuries. They are structural necessities. This is the premise behind the manifesto: that the most future-ready investors will not be those who know the most, but those who *know themselves best*—and act accordingly.

So write your manifesto. Make it portable. Make it honest. And make it resilient. Because markets will always evolve. But *principles should not require rebalancing.*

# Conclusion
# Investing as a Human Act

What does it mean—truly mean—to invest with intelligence, with conscience, with care, in a world now increasingly sculpted by machines?

No matter how seamless the interface, how sophisticated the code, how eerily precise the prediction—investing, at its root, remains a distinctly human act. The mechanisms shift, yes. Data streams swell. Brokers yield ground to algorithms. But behind it all, there is always someone choosing. A preference, a conviction, a hunch perhaps—or simply a flicker of hope. This is not a trivial detail buried beneath technological sophistication. It is, if anything, the heart of the matter.

And so here we are, at the close of the arc, circling back to the foundational question that quietly threads through all that's come before: what does it actually *mean* to invest, now that machines aren't merely assisting, but increasingly shaping the landscape in which decisions unfold? We've moved beyond the "how" and "where" of capital allocation. Even the "what" feels insufficient. The true question pushes further inward: *why* do we invest at all? And in doing so, what sort of world are we choosing to bring forth?

Let's be honest—we're not spectators in this age of automation. We are its collaborators. Sometimes reluctantly, sometimes enthusiastically, but always participants. And with that participation comes responsibility. Moral responsibility, even.

To reduce investing to a dry chase for return is to miss the point entirely. Do that, and you're not making judgments—you're just solving equations. But meaningful investing asks for more than maths. It requires discernment. It requires that we weigh values against outcomes, futures against fears, profit against principle. It is, at its most honest, an act of belief. A quiet, potent declaration about the kind of world we're willing to support—and the one we'd rather not.

Here, at this threshold, technology finds its limits. Machines can compute. They can identify patterns we'd never notice, act faster than we'd dare, and operate without fatigue or bias—well, without human bias. But they cannot answer the moral questions. They do not know what's worth preserving. They cannot decide whether a company heals or harms, whether a policy empowers or excludes, whether a community thrives or decays. These aren't code problems. They're human dilemmas.

And outcomes—real, messy, irreversible outcomes—still belong to us. They always will.

### The Central Risk of a Machine-Driven Market: Moral Abdication

Perhaps the greatest risk in an AI-optimised financial system is not systemic collapse or volatility spikes—it is *moral abdication.* The danger that, in offloading our thinking to machines, we also offload our judgment. That we begin to see "what the model suggests" as an excuse to disengage from ethical discernment.

The investor of the future must resist this temptation. Automation should enhance wisdom, not replace it. It should expand our vantage point, not absolve us of responsibility. To invest without reflecting on *impact*, *context*, or *consequence* is not sophistication. It is negligence dressed as efficiency.

### From Investor to Architect

If we accept that investing is a form of participation, then we must also accept that investors are not just market actors—they are *architects* of the future. Every trade is a signal. Every allocation a choice. Every holding a hypothesis about what deserves to grow.

Investors influence which business models thrive. Which environmental practices are normalised. Which governance standards are rewarded. In aggregate, markets are not neutral. They are *mirrors of our collective attention and incentives.*

This does not mean one must become a moral absolutist to participate in capital markets. It does mean that values matter. That *ethical intentionality*—however personally defined—must be integrated into how we assess opportunity and risk. The future will belong not to those who optimise blindly, but to those who ask the harder questions.

### Human Intelligence: The Irreplaceable Layer

Across the previous chapters, we've explored AI as a tool—powerful, adaptive, increasingly indispensable. But tools are only as effective as the hands that wield them. And here's the paradox: the more advanced AI becomes, the more essential it is for investors to cultivate distinctly human forms of intelligence.

Critical thinking. Emotional regulation. Systems-level reasoning. Moral clarity. These are not soft skills. They are *strategic imperatives*. In a world where machines can surface any signal, the question becomes: *which signal do you choose to act on?* That is a human decision.

Moreover, the cultivation of such human faculties is not static. It is ongoing. A lifelong discipline. Not unlike investing itself.

### Investment as Attention

There's an overlooked truth here: investment is not only the deployment of capital—it is the *allocation of attention*. What we study, what we track, what we deem "material" or "immaterial" shapes what we notice. And what we notice shapes what we act on.

The implication is profound. If we allow our attention to be captured solely by machine-curated dashboards and volatility indexes, we risk internalising the belief that *only what can be measured matters*. But *much of what drives long-term value creation cannot be neatly modelled.* Culture. Trust. Leadership integrity. Ecosystem resilience. These are not spreadsheet variables—but they are investment fundamentals.

The act of being present with one's investment decisions—of pausing to consider *why* an asset is attractive, *how* it aligns with personal values, *what* trade-offs are being accepted—is not inefficient. It is the core of what makes investing meaningful.

## Participation Beyond Profit

Profit is necessary. It enables growth, sustains innovation, and compensates risk. But *profit alone is an incomplete definition of success.* A market can be efficient and still be extractive. A portfolio can outperform and still misalign with one's convictions. The question investors must ask is not just "how much did I make?" but *"what did my capital make possible?"*

This reframing invites a broader definition of wealth—one that includes financial return, certainly, but also social impact, environmental sustainability, and personal alignment. It proposes that the true mark of investment success is not just the size of the return, but the *quality of its consequence.*

## Closing the Loop: Investing as a Human Act

To invest is to believe in the future. Not with blind optimism, but with pragmatic engagement. Not with technocratic detachment, but with ethical presence.

This book has taken you through models, strategies, risks, tools, and frameworks. But its purpose was always more ambitious: to reconnect intelligence with intention. To help you reimagine investing not as a series of technical moves, but as *a human practice*—one that sits at the intersection of reason and responsibility, ambition and humility, innovation and conscience.

The investor of the future will not be the one with the most data. It will be the one with the clearest lens. The ability to integrate insight and value, to act with conviction in uncertainty, and to design portfolios that reflect not just market wisdom, but human presence.

That is what it means to invest in a world run by machines. Not to compete with them. Not to surrender to them. But to *collaborate*—intelligently, ethically, and intentionally.

Let that be your edge.

Let that be your legacy.

## Investing as a Human Act

*Reclaiming Judgement, Ethics, and Presence in an Age of Automated Finance*

If you strip away the noise—the dashboards, the forecasts, the algorithms, the media cycles—what remains at the heart of investing is this: *a decision made by a human, with a stake in the future.* No amount of machine learning alters that basic truth. And yet, the illusion that we can—or should—outsource meaning to machines has never been more seductive. This chapter is not an argument against technology. It is a defence of *discernment.*

Let's be clear: artificial intelligence has radically improved what investors can analyse, monitor, and model. Quant tools can identify patterns humans miss. Sentiment models scrape millions of posts and parse them in milliseconds. Portfolio management platforms optimise exposures with a level of precision that would have been unimaginable a decade ago. And still, despite these advancements, the central question persists: *what does it mean to invest wisely in a world run by machines?*

Because efficiency is not wisdom. Automation is not integrity. And intelligence—no matter how artificial—is not a substitute for *intent.*

### Profit as an Insufficient Goal

There's nothing inherently wrong with pursuing profit. Return on capital is how ideas get funded, innovation scales, and retirement accounts grow. But when profit becomes the only goal—when metrics override meaning—investing risks degenerating into a form of *economic nihilism.* A kind of ultra-rational detachment where what matters is *what works*, regardless of *what it affects.*

The question "Will this investment grow?" must coexist with "Should this investment grow?" That's not idealism. It's realism informed by responsibility.

Consider the ripple effects of investment capital: which companies get fuelled, which industries are reshaped, which behaviours are rewarded. Investing isn't neutral. It's participatory. Every trade is a signal, every allocation a vote—often unconscious, sometimes misaligned, but always consequential.

So what happens when those decisions are increasingly shaped by AI systems optimised for performance, not principle?

### The Temptation of Automation, and the Price of Abdication

There is a creeping danger in high-frequency, high-efficiency investing: *the erosion of moral agency.* Not because investors consciously choose to be unethical, but because the machinery of markets makes it so easy not to think.

Models are consulted. Dashboards glow. The decision is made. And slowly, imperceptibly, the human recedes into the background. The question of "why" becomes secondary to "how fast" and "how much." The craft of investing—long synonymous with judgment and philosophy—risks being reduced to *a lever pulled by default.*

But decisions made without reflection are not neutral. They are shaped by the data they consume, the incentives they encode, and the assumptions they fail to question. AI is not immune to these biases. It reflects them—often with extraordinary confidence.

This is where the human investor must reclaim their role—not just as user of tools, but as *custodian of intent.*

**Participation Requires Presence**

What does it mean to be *present* in your investments?

It means understanding that every asset represents something real—a company, a product, a workforce, a footprint, a future. It means asking: *what am I underwriting with my capital? Whose story am I funding? What vision am I scaling?*

It means acknowledging that risk is not just volatility, but consequence. That return is not just a percentage, but a footprint. That diversification is not merely exposure to asset classes, but exposure to values.

This level of attentiveness demands something machines cannot offer: *moral discernment.* Not the rote ethics of ESG filters, but the deeper practice of aligning your investment strategy with your worldview. And that, invariably, is a human act.

**Why Human Intelligence Still Matters**

In a saturated tech landscape, many investors are tempted to believe that their edge must come from data: better models, faster signals, more granular insights. But as access to those tools becomes increasingly commoditised, the real edge will shift.

The winning investors of the future will not be those who know *more*, but those who know *better*. Who can contextualise data with judgment. Who can separate noise from signal not just statistically, but philosophically.

They will be people who ask different questions. Who reflect longer. Who act with intention in a world that incentivises speed.

This doesn't mean rejecting technology. It means *integrating it intelligently*. Leveraging AI to enhance your reach while maintaining your grip on the wheel. Knowing when to trust the model—and when to override it.

### Case in Point: Markets Misreading the Moment

Look at the recent mispricing of sustainability transitions. For years, markets rewarded fossil fuel incumbents for short-term earnings while penalising long-term clean energy bets. Algorithms trained on historical data reinforced this logic—until regulatory, geopolitical, and climate tipping points converged. Suddenly, the so-called "irrational idealists" looked like prescient risk managers. The lesson? *No model can account for moral momentum—until it's too late.*

### Reframing the Goal: Wealth as Stewardship

We must also ask what wealth is *for.* If the endgame is merely accumulation, then markets become extraction machines. But if wealth is understood as *a form of stewardship*—of ideas, of communities, of shared futures—then investing becomes not just a financial act, but a civic one.

This doesn't require abandoning performance. It requires *expanding the definition of performance.* To include durability. Fairness. Transparency. Intergenerational relevance.

Investors who grasp this shift are not sacrificing alpha. They are *future-proofing their portfolios by aligning them with durable societal trends*—the demand for accountability, sustainability, and purpose.

### Building a Philosophy of Practice

The investor who treats capital as agency—not just arithmetic—must cultivate a new discipline: *philosophical intentionality*. This doesn't mean reading Plato. It means defining what you stand for—and how your investments reflect it.

It means journaling your decisions, reviewing your assumptions, revising your principles when new truths emerge. It means setting filters not just for risk, but for meaning.

Above all, it means seeing investing not as a series of technical bets, but as a moral practice conducted in real time, with real stakes.

## Machines Can Optimise. Only Humans Can Care.

This is the ultimate distinction. AI can recommend, simulate, even execute. But it cannot care. It cannot define meaning. It cannot choose *what matters*.

Only you can do that.

And that responsibility—far from being a burden—is a privilege. It's what transforms investing from a mechanical process into a human one. It's what makes markets more than mechanisms. It's what allows finance to be not just efficient, but *ethical*.

## Final Reflections: You Are the Algorithm Now

Here's the quiet truth: the most powerful algorithm in your portfolio is *you*. Your values. Your judgment. Your capacity to think beyond the dashboard.

You determine the questions worth asking. The time horizons worth holding. The signals worth trusting. You define the boundary between what is actionable and what is wise.

The future of investing will be shaped not only by what we can automate, but by what we *choose* not to.

Let that be your standard.

Let that be your signal.

Let that be your contribution to a more intelligent, ethical, and human future.

# About the Author

Dr. Elias van Rothenstein is a global financial futurist and behavioural economist who bridges the worlds of technology, philosophy, and wealth strategy. With a background in neuroeconomics and AI systems design, he has advised institutional investors, start-ups, and governments on how to navigate complex financial ecosystems in a rapidly digitising world. Known for his provocative insights and interdisciplinary research, Elias redefines what it means to be a modern investor—grounded in human judgment, yet fluent in machine intelligence. His work challenges assumptions, dismantles outdated paradigms, and equips readers to make deeply intentional financial choices in an age of relentless innovation.

www.ingramcontent.com/pod-product-compliance
Lightning Source LLC
Chambersburg PA
CBHW031342230926
51848CB00002B/347